Copyright © 2023 Les Stanley

The moral right of the author has been asserted.
All rights reserved. No part of this publication may be reproduced, or transmitted by any person or entity (including Google, Amazon or similar organisations), in any form or by any means electronic or mechanical, including photocopying, recording, scanning or by any information storage and retrieval system or transmitted in any form, or by any means without the prior written permission without prior permission in writing from the publisher.

A CIP catalogue record for this book is available from the National Library of Australia.

E-Book - Kindle

978-0-6451358-9-3

Paperback

978-0-6486607-7-4

Front Cover Picture Provided By Chow
Cover Design by Nabinkarna on Fiverr

www.lesstanley.com

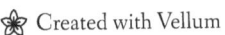

Mostly Fun

Soft Nut Bike Tours of Laos and Thailand

Les Stanley

Foreward by Jeff Stoward

The title *Mostly Fun - The Soft Nut Bike Tours of Laos and Thailand*, accurately captures the essence of this engaging and insightful read, yet a more fitting title would be *The Wandering Whinger: A Pythonic Pedal Through the Tropics*.

The author, Les, an endearingly oblivious middle-aged Pom, hilariously narrates his misadventures amidst enchanting landscapes, astride his trusty bicycle. From battling rogue customs officers to eccentric travel companions, this absurdly witty tale embraces cultural clashes, bicycle blunders, medical misfortunes, and quintessential British grumbling about everything else under the sun. Les suffered so that we didn't have to, so really, he's like a Jesus character to me. "Christ on a Bike" - perhaps that should have been the book's title? Regardless, it's an absolute riot to read!

Praise for Mostly Fun.

Les has that rare ability of seamlessly transporting the reader to a specific time and place, without charging you for a plane ticket. This latest memoir of adventures in Thailand and Laos brings all the colour of Southeast Asia to life, giving insight into the character of local people and fellow travellers, the feel of life on the road and where to find the region's best beer.

— Jack Jordan - Senior Financial and Shipping Journalist

Les Stanley has done it again! Once more we are invited into the sardonic explorer's trips to exotic backwaters that take him on hilarious digressions down the quirky alleys of his anti-heroic past. It's a drily comic, sideways look at the world from the point of view of a grumpy adventurer with a healthy quotient of self-mockery.

— David Stoyle - Researcher in Literature

Praise for Mostly Fun.

at the University of the Côte d'Azur, Nice
France

This book is as funny as buggery. I was happy when I'd finished it.

— Chris Adams - French Tutor

Map of Thailand and Laos

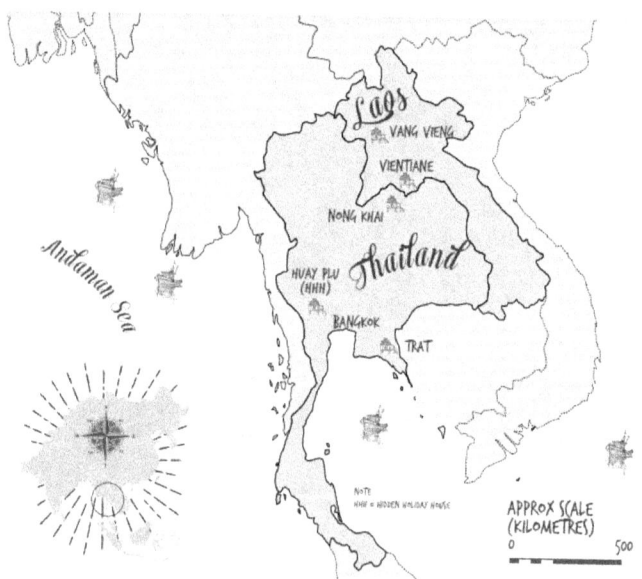

Map showing main locations visited in Mostly Fun

Contents

Foreward by Jeff Stoward	1
Praise for Mostly Fun.	2
Map of Thailand and Laos	4

Part One

Surviving Christmas	11
Post-Christmas Chill and a Happy New Year	15
Pre-Flight Nerves	17
Departure Day	20

Part Two

Bike Trip 1 - Central Laos	25
One Night in Bangkok	27
What's in a Name?	29
A Tale of Two Breakfasts	32
Across the Borderline	34
The M25 of Vientiane	38
I Still Need to Lie Down	40
A Week of Chinese New Years	44
A Boat, A Train, A Massage	47
To Ride or Not to Ride	53
A Day to Myself	57
On the Train	60
Promenade, Passaggiare, Spaziergang	63
Around Vientiane	66
Back Over the Border	70
Dinner Choices	72
To Cargo or Not to Cargo, This is the Station	75

Part Three

Quiet Days at HHH	79
Contemplation	80
Temples and Markets	82
Living Next Door to Alice	88

Part Four

Quiet Days In Bangkok	93
Inane Conversations with Taxi Drivers - An Avoidance Strategy	94
Don't Believe the Reviews	97
Early Check Out	104
To Thai or not to Thai	107
A Walk in the Park	109
The Det 5 Story	113
Bongo, Bongo	115
Down Memory Lane	117
Let the Train Take the Strain	120
Dining on the Observation Deck	124
Bars of Bangkok	127
Shopping	129
Tom's Diner	131
Bangkok Backwards	133
Spicy, Funny	138
Burger King, Hungry Jack's	140

Part Five

Bike Trip 2 - Eastern Thailand	145
On the Road Again	146
More Meandering in the Mangroves	151
My View on Philosophy	154
Tackling the Hills	159
Gems and Beer	161
The Fast Route to Paradise	167
A Trip to Chanthaburi Cathedral	170
The Man Who Didn't Love Islands	172

Escape from Alcatraz	177
Look at Trat	180
Bangkok Traffic	182

Part Six

Quiet Days In Huay Phlu	187
Best Laid Plans	188
Going Up the Country	190
Trains, and Trains, and Trains	192
One Big Fantasy	194
Kids? - Nein Danke	196
Epilogue	198
Autumn Fall	199
About the Author	205
Cannes Encore! Travel in the Time of COVID	207
The Soft Nut Bike Tour of Burma	209
My Brother's Bicycle	211
Photos from the Road	213

Part One

Surviving Christmas

It's 25 December, Christmas Day. Church bells are ringing in the distance to remind everyone what day it is. The calm before the storm. I'm waiting to start a day of eating too much and listening to stories of people, some dead and some still living, whom I have never met. I'm also thinking about my upcoming trip to Thailand and Laos. Flights are booked, visas applied for and a bunch of things I don't really need have been purchased. I think back to my early travelling days when I would blithely throw a few mismatched clothes into a cheap backpack, along with a toothbrush, and head off.

That's not 100% true. For my much dreamed of "overland to India" trip, I wandered the streets of London for weeks looking for the perfect backpack, sleeping bag and boots. Back in the late 70s the main area to find these items was around The Strand, where the YHA (Youth Hostels Association) had their headquarters. I spent many an hour in Millets and other long gone "travel goods" stores, scouring the shelves for bargains. Quite why I thought I needed mountain climbing gear to sit on trains and buses as I crossed the Asian sub-continent I don't know. I suppose, in the back of my mind, I had some vague inkling of a plan that I would visit Nepal and The Himalayas where they would be useful. But, during the trip, for the most part, the hefty boots I purchased were more of a hindrance than a help.

But back to the future. In three weeks, I'll board a plane from Brisbane bound for Bangkok via Singapore. Two bike trips are planned. One in Laos, and, a week or so later, one in Thailand itself. I know I'll be one of the oldest people on both trips and probably the least fit. I'm trying not to let this fact intimidate me too much. For these trips, after many years of travelling, I like to think I have packed more sensibly. Despite that, I also know that, when I get home, there'll be at least one item I didn't need. Probably a shirt that it was either too hot or too cold to wear.

Christmas day passed. I tried hard to think of a Christmas day I'd enjoyed in the last 50 years or more. Up until the age of 11 or 12, Christmas was great. Presents, special food, Morecambe and Wise. Then I became capable of original thought. I recalled a couple of Christmases I had enjoyed since becoming a teenager. There was one year when I worked for an airline and had the opportunity to do a shift on the phones on Christmas day. I jumped at the chance. Triple pay, and we could drink wine, illicitly I imagine, while our customers, mostly Americans and people from The Middle East, called up with bizarre requests.

Another time was when I was a volunteer on a kibbutz in Israel. We worked Christmas day, but had Boxing Day off. Or maybe it was just Saturday, it was a few years ago. We volunteers were given access to an old shed to hold a celebration. We worked hard over the weeks beforehand, cleaning it up and, if I remember correctly, even painting the walls. A small concert was organised and, hoping it might be my introduction to fame and fortune, I wrote a Pythonesque skit, to be performed by myself and two of my buddies.

The basic premise of the skit was that the volunteer manager was greeting a couple of new volunteers. The actual volunteer manager was a north London lady with whom I had, just a few days previously, had issues, due to what I saw as unfair allocation of duties. I was to play her part, while my buddies were the recently arrived newcomers. In a flash of inspiration, on the way to The Shed, I had picked up a couple of fallen palm fronds and decided to wear them as a wig. This stroke of genius probably got the biggest laugh of the evening.

I only remember one line of the script, which went something like:

- I'd offer you a cigarette but I've only got 19 left.

I've also enjoyed the times I've been on my own at Christmas. Just me and a pizza with ice cream for dessert, washed down with a nice bottle of red. No feigning joy at unwanted gifts, no carols or any other insipid Christmas music. In the afternoon, a couple of Star Trek - The Next Generation obviously - episodes as my lunch digests followed by a nap. Such a perfect day, I'm glad I spent it with me.

Post-Christmas Chill and a Happy New Year

After spending most of Christmas day in near arctic conditions, due to the low setting of the air-conditioning, I felt I was coming down with a chill. Sore throat, runny nose etc. I took a COVID test and was pleased it was negative.

Over the next few days, the period between Christmas and New Year that a friend of mine calls *Amateur Drunk Week*, I was still not feeling great. Another friend suggested drinking all day as an antidote. I went for the healthy choice and lazed around the house, watching Star Trek. The days passed and I began to feel better but there was still New Years Eve to endure. I struggle to remember ever enjoying this particular celebration either. As a child, of course, I was always fast asleep in bed by midnight. There were a couple of parties I attended as a teenager, and into my 20s, but my main recollection is of being rejected by any female I tried to befriend. That, and immediately hearing:

- Stanley, you tosser, leave it alone,

when I tried to commandeer the record player and put on a Cream or Black Sabbath album. This also happened when I selected James Taylor, Carole King or Joni Mitchell, the triumvirate of late 60s and early 70s music excellence.

- Stanley, you tosser, what's that boring shit?

my doltish, musically moronic, Top of the Pops educated, pals would shout. Eventually, I would usually find a quiet corner and try to stay awake until it was all over at midnight. I'd sit, silently swigging from a Watney's Party 7 until around 10:00pm and then I'd wait, and wait, for the countdown; 5, 4, 3, 2, 1, Happy New Year! Maybe there were a couple of years in my 20s when I enjoyed the evening, if only because it meant the possibility of some physical contact with a girl. But, it's all such a long time ago.

New Year, 2022 passed without incident. I was aware of some fireworks around 8:30pm, just before I went to bed. I was awoken from a peaceful slumber again at midnight. I lay awake for a few moments, as the explosions sounded, thinking, just a couple of days to go before I board my flight to Bangkok via Singapore. I'd packed and repacked a few times and was, by now, pretty sure I had all I'd need. Of course, somewhere along the way I knew I'd realised I had forgotten something important.

Pre-Flight Nerves

As always, I was a bit agitated for a few days before departure. I think most people are. As the day drew nearer, I'd drift off to sleep each night having my standard pre-trip fantasy - no not that one - about hyper-fast trains that ran at around Mach 5, approaching 4000 kms an hour, between Brisbane, Australia and wherever my destination might be. Running in vacuum tunnels, on Maglev tracks, there was no turbulence, in fact very little real sense of movement at all. Accelerating at a comfortable rate of 10 km an hour every 10 seconds, they would reach their cruising speed in just over an hour. Brisbane to Bangkok, in less than four hours; time for a drink, a nap, a movie, a quick shower – of course they'd have showers, and another drink before arrival. These trains would be equipped with comfortable seating and areas where you could stretch out and sleep. Restaurants and a bar, perhaps even a massage room. One day, one day.

. . .

I knew that, once I was on my way, I'd settle down. It doesn't seem to matter how much travelling I do, there's always something to be concerned about. When I was younger, this didn't happen. I'd just casually turn up at a bus station, train station, ferry terminal or occasionally even an airport, quite unconcerned about conditions and requirements at my destination, where I was going and what the trip would be like. No lengthy investigations of facilities available on either departure or arrival, no checking weather maps, no idea of what I would need/have to do on arrival. Google may make our lives easier in many ways but it has also removed almost any element of surprise and discovery from travelling.

Even as I prepared for the impending trip, I was planning another, later the same year. Starting with Bangkok of course, then on to Istanbul, a train or two through south-eastern Europe to Vienna, where I would stay a week or two practising my German. Then, down to Nice and Southern France and Italy before crossing the length of France, with a stop in Paris and ending up in London.

Things get a little vague after that. The intention is to spend Christmas with my nephew Tom who lives in Hong Kong. Who knows, maybe I'll even enjoy this one?

From Bangkok I want to travel overland to Vietnam via Cambodia. This was a trip I always meant to do when I lived in Bangkok, but people kept dying. My plan was to use three of my paltry four weeks annual leave to complete the journey. This never happened as, every couple of years, a close relative left this earthly realm and my plans were scuppered. Instead of taking the train from Bangkok to the Cambodian border, I'd instead board a flight to England to attend their funeral and dutifully stand by their grave at the cemetery, or watch them disappear behind a curtain at the crematorium.

Departure Day

The day to leave Brisbane for Bangkok finally arrived. I was, as always, at the airport early, and after checking in, wandered around desperate for something to do. Mostly without success as I had no need to buy any Billabong, Rip-Curl, or R M Williams branded clothing. I also passed on the dried kangaroo meat and chocolate-coated macadamias.

Brief excitement ensued when my name was called just before boarding and I was sure I had been upgraded. But no, this was only to check that I spoke English and could be called upon to open the emergency exit, as I was seated in an exit row. I enjoyed the flight, even if it was one of the bumpiest I have ever taken. Breathing exercises, mild meditation and drugs, alleviated any nausea. Wondering how you open an emergency exit also helped pass the time.

. . .

Departure Day

As I'd paid a bit extra for my exit row seat, I had plenty of legroom and, even though the lady behind me was unable to stand up without grabbing the back of my seat and shaking it vigorously, the flight went well enough. "Maybe she's an alien," I thought, "from a low-gravity world". I always like to give people the benefit of the doubt.

On arrival in Bangkok, I strode, head held high, past the taxi touts, fought my way through the group tour throngs who always seemed to stand huddled in any available space, waiting for instructions as to what to do next, and made my way to the ground floor where I knew the train to the city departed. I loved taking the train from the airport, any airport really. The feeling of independence was wonderful. It also negated the need to risk my life in a taxi, or be engaged in some meaningless conversation with the driver.

Part Two

Bike Trip 1 - Central Laos

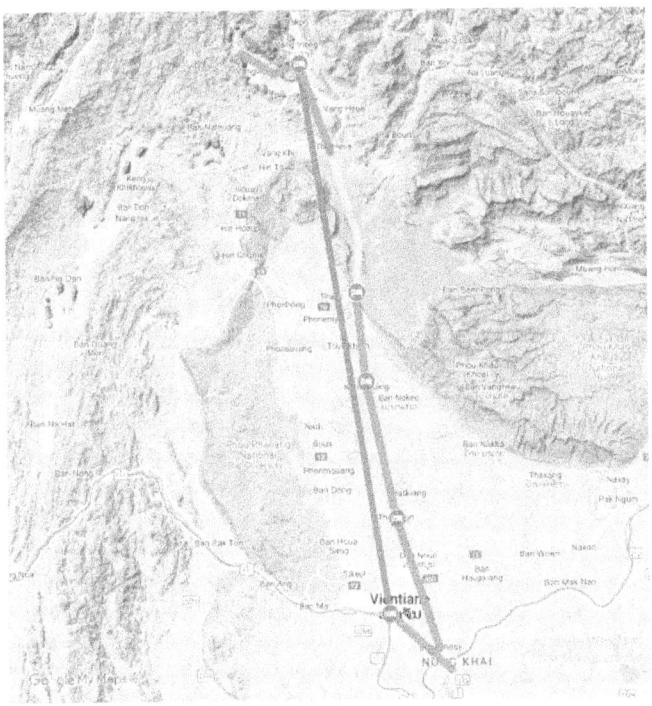

The curvy line shows our bike route in Laos. The straight one shows the route the train took on the return

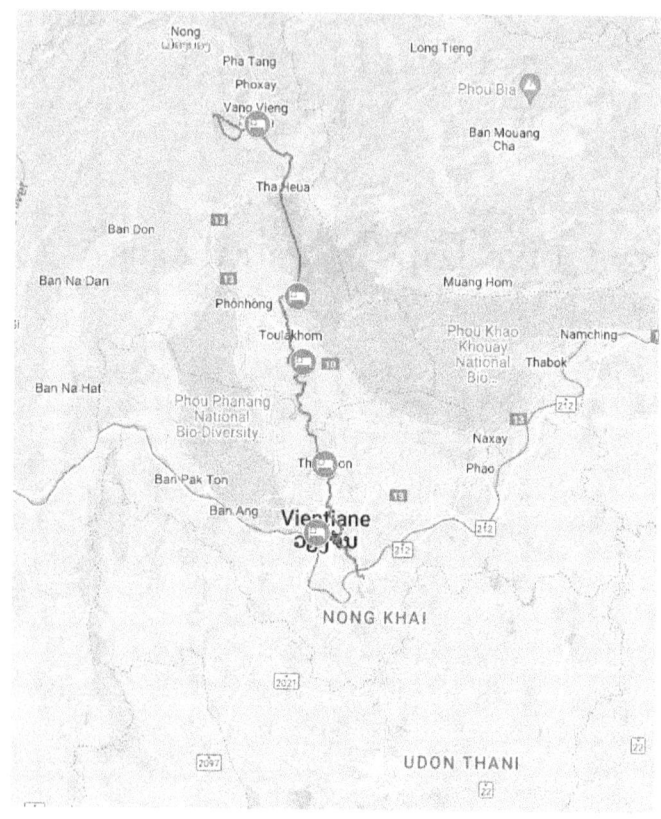

Our cycling route in detail including stops

One Night in Bangkok

I slept well enough on my first night in Bangkok, until 03.30am when I was wide awake and ready to start the day. I amused myself with YouTube and dozed a little until around 06:00am when I finally got up and went to the small hotel gym for some exercise. Later I nipped out for a haircut and pedicure at a barbershop run by an old Chinese guy who had been there forever. His cosy shop is located in an area better known for other services and, even at 10:00am, I was offered something other than a haircut by the friendly ladies next door. My next stop was the bank where I had some financial transactions to sort out.

A few hours later, I made my way to the station to meet the other people on the trip. Bangkok Hualamphong station was still operating but most long-distance trains had recently made the move to depart from a new station to the north of the city at Bang Sue. When I say recently, I mean they were beginning operations from that day.

Our train to Nong Khai, near the border with Laos, was delayed, and delayed. I suppose, as this was the first day of operations from this station, I should not have been too surprised.

The name of the station is a story in itself. Most people refer to it as Bang Sue Grand Station due to its location adjacent to the already existing Bang Sue station. Officially though, it's called Krung Thep Aphiwat Central Terminal. Krung Thep, itself an abbreviation, is the actual Thai name of Bangkok. Aphiwat is difficult to translate precisely, but means something like blessed, hallowed or sacred.

Finally, the train departed, moving fast on the new line out of the city. After a few catch-up conversations with those I knew from previous trips and getting to know any new joiners, I settled down behind my curtain hoping to sleep. Thai trains are comfortable enough but for safety reasons they keep the carriage lights on full all night. This is apparently done to avoid accidents when people climb down from the top bunks. But I really felt as if I was in some kind of interrogation chamber all night and slept fitfully. Later, on my return journey, which was also overnight, I realised that, by ensuring the curtain of the top bunk was properly closed I could eliminate most of the tortuous light.

What's in a Name?

Knowing that part of writing any account of a trip with other people consists of describing them and their actions and, not wanting to openly vilify, denigrate or insult any of my co-cyclists, some people will be referred to by nicknames, as follows:

Chris - not a nickname at all but our fearless leader. I've known Chris for many years and have no intention of saying anything even vaguely negative about him.

Areeya - Chris's wife. An equally wonderful person who requires no nickname.

Uncle Fred - I've used this name to describe one of the other cyclists as he shared a hairstyle and, in some ways, a personality with my own late, Uncle Fred.

. . .

The Dutchman - I never worked out if he was Dutch or Belgian. Or why he'd somehow been in the German army and spoke German.

This is probably as good a time as any to compare my thoughts on group versus single travel. When I started travelling the world, I could not imagine ever going on any kind of group tour. Even travelling with a girlfriend or other companion had its downsides.

In my previous book, *My Brother's Bicycle,* I've described the various petty disagreements Alan, my fellow adventurer, and I had over certain things. In reality, these were few and far between, as I generally just went along with whatever harebrained scheme he cooked up. I like to think I'm a fairly flexible travel partner, but I'm not sure those who have travelled with me would agree. On the journeys described in this book, I had the best of both worlds.

The bike trips themselves had been organised by my friend Chris, who does a fantastic job. For all tours, he'd first go on a scouting trip, usually covering in one day what we would later cover in two or three. Apart from exploring the most interesting routes, he also investigated options for accommodation and places to eat. On the trips themselves, he'll happily negotiate strange dietary requirements and other urgent needs, such as cold beer, for participants. On top of this should someone fall sick, or simply not have the stamina to complete a day on their bike, Chris can be relied upon to find some alternative means of transport for the unfortunate one. He keeps the groups fairly small, usually no more than 10 people. So, there is less chance of anyone too special joining. Not that it hasn't happened.

In between the two bike trips, I also had 10 days to myself. I knew I would have no problem filling this time. This had not always been the case on some of my previous journeys. I remembered many long days, lying on lumpy beds in cheap hotel rooms, with only a much thumbed paperback for company. On those days, where time dragged slowly, I would try and console myself by contemplating one of Henry's quotes:

To be silent the whole day long, see no newspaper, hear no radio, listen to no gossip, be thoroughly and completely lazy, thoroughly and completely indifferent to the fate of the world is the finest medicine a man can give himself.

These days, except in the most desolate parts of the globe, one is never really completely cut-off. The internet is always with you. This makes it difficult to isolate oneself from the world's goings on. But some days I like to try.

A Tale of Two Breakfasts

Day 1 – Nong Khai to Tha Ngon – 39km biking, elevation gain 225m

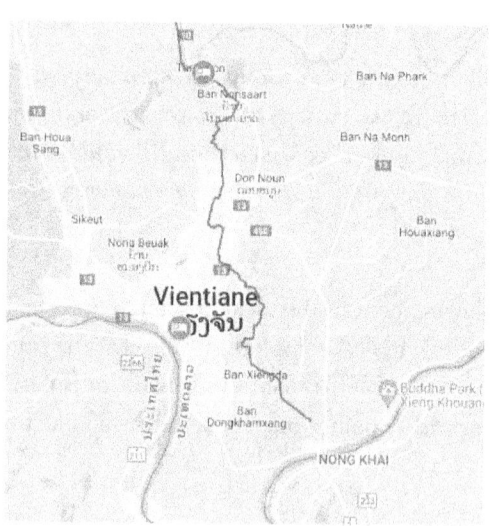

Off the train we cross the border, avoid the Vientiane traffic and head north

A Tale of Two Breakfasts

I was wide awake around 05:30am, and ravenously hungry as I, and therefore my digestive system, was still three hours ahead, on Brisbane time. Fortunately, breakfast was available on the train and I tucked in to a plastic tray of fried eggs and chips. Not a very Thai breakfast, but I was hungry and it tasted delicious. An hour or so later we pulled into Nong Khai and were pleased to see our bikes, which had had to travel on another train for logistical reasons. Also waiting on the station were a few other people who were joining the trip there.

We checked our bikes, loaded our bags and rode a few kilometres to a local restaurant for a second breakfast. The choices here were far more Thai, with the friendly owner offering various types of noodle soup. There was a solitary western guy there, a teacher at a nearby school, who turned out to be Canadian. His hopes of a quiet breakfast were shattered as he was assailed by questions from the over inquisitive new arrivals.

Across the Borderline

After our second breakfast, and the inquisition of the lonely diner, we struck out for the border. To cross from Thailand into Laos, one goes over the Friendship Bridge. The actual border is halfway across the bridge, or, more correctly, in the middle of the river which runs beneath it. But setting up customs posts and the other paraphernalia needed to cross from one country to the next there would not be practical, so the actual border crossing is situated on the Laos side of the bridge. We rode across, jockeying for space with cars and, more concerningly, diesel-fuming trucks. There was also a pedestrian path which was quite wide and I wondered why we had not ridden on that. Surely it would have been safer. As we approached the halfway mark, and therefore the actual border, I realised why. The entire pedestrian path was blocked by a high concrete wall. Obviously there to stop the locals wandering into the wrong country. We continued on as the flags placed every 100 metres changed from the red white and blue stripes of Thailand, to the similarly hued, but differently designed one of Laos.

As with many border crossings, much filling out of forms, waiting in queues and answering inane questions, was required. Additionally, in Asia at least, there's always a requirement to talk to someone through a tiny glass window, located far too low for anyone over 5 feet tall. As we were travelling with "vehicles" we also had to fill out a form with their details. The form was, of course, really designed for those crossing with cars or trucks, not bikes. Under name of vehicle, to amuse myself, I wrote *Ethel*. Apart from the time-wasting bureaucracy, the crossing went fairly smoothly and, after an hour, or so we were waved out of Thailand and into Laos by a friendly young woman in a uniform two sizes too big for her. Once on the Laos side we had a few things to do; money changing, SIM purchasing, beverage and ice cream shopping. As we were a group of 10 all of this took time. I'd completed my exchanges and purchases and was looking for a place to stand out of the sun when a more official looking border guard than the diminutive young lady we had encountered previously, approached us:

  - *You must come back,* he said, *something wrong.*

We considered making a run for it. After all, we had already crossed the border and could have just jumped on our bikes and ridden off. I doubt the slightly overweight border guard would have been able to catch us. However, a group of 10, mostly foreign, cyclists would have been easy to spot on the road and no doubt the Laos authorities would have caught up with us sooner rather than later. Also, the border guard had a gun.

We rode obediently back towards the border crossing point. The young woman was still there, looking a little uncomfortable. I assumed she'd been admonished for letting us through so easily. For the next 30 minutes a complicated discussion ensued. It took place in a mixture of English, Lao and Thai. Our crime, it seemed, was that two of the group were Thai citizens. One was Areeya, Chris's wife, so obviously she would be returning to Thailand. The fact that Chris and Areeya were riding a tandem made this fact even more of a certainty. But there was another Thai national among us, and the Lao authorities had the ridiculous idea that she was planning to sell her bike in Laos, and then hightail it back to Thailand with the loot, cunningly avoiding any sales tax.

It was all quite farcical, and when the subject of "insurance" came up we realised the whole escapade was nothing but a ruse to get some money out of us. Further discussion took place, until we all agreed to pay the princely sum of 100 Thai baht (around A$5.00) for the "insurance". A wad of notes changed hands and Chris was given a handwritten note, with an official stamp, to prove we had paid the insurance. Transaction over, we rode back passed the banks and phone shops and began our real adventure in Laos.

Across the Borderline

. . .

In the itinerary we'd all been sent before the trip started, there was a plan to take the train which runs from Nong Khai, across the border, terminating on the Laos side at Tha Naleng. In fact, until very recently, when the link between Boten on the Chinese border and Vientiane, Laos' capital was built, it was the only train line in the whole country. The line is being extended to Vientiane South train station and this segment was due to be opened by the end of 2022. But the opening of the new station had been delayed and the decision made to ride over the border instead.

The M25 of Vientiane

We rode through the outskirts of Vientiane. We would be staying there for a day on the way back, so there would be plenty of time to explore the city then. After a short detour at a small lake to admire the view, we pedalled on to the newly built Laos National Museum. We stopped here to learn some history of the country we were going to spend the next few days biking through. The place was well air-conditioned and a wonderful escape from the steadily building heat. After all the hanging around and other complications at the border, in addition to the 20 or so kilometres we had already cycled, all I really wanted to do was sit, or even better, lie down. Preferably under a fan. I forced myself to show some interest and wandered through the exhibits for a while. Most of these were wood carvings of important events in the history of the country.

The highlight of the visit for me, was a ride in an elevator which had no functioning lights. I only realised it had no lights once the doors had slid shut and I was plunged into absolute darkness. Fortunately, I had already pressed the button for the ground floor so I stood, not daring to move, while the contraption slowly made its way down. The journey took no more than 15 seconds but I was relieved when we reached our destination and the doors slid open, filling the space with light.

On exiting the building, I found that The Dutchman and his lovely wife, had also seen enough and were lying on the ground, in the only bit of shade available, quietly dozing. How I envied them. Another hour or so of riding through more rural scenery brought us to to the town of Tha Ngon, located at a bend of the Nam Ngum river, where we checked into our hotel. This town is well known locally for its floating restaurants. After a brief rest and well needed shower, we made our way onto one of the restaurant rafts which floated along the river while we enjoyed our dinner and the views. Fortunately, there was no loud thumping music on our boat, but the noise of the diesel engine compensated, and made conversation a challenge.

I Still Need to Lie Down

*Day 2 – Tha Ngon to Ban Keaun – 43km
biking, elevation gain 221m*

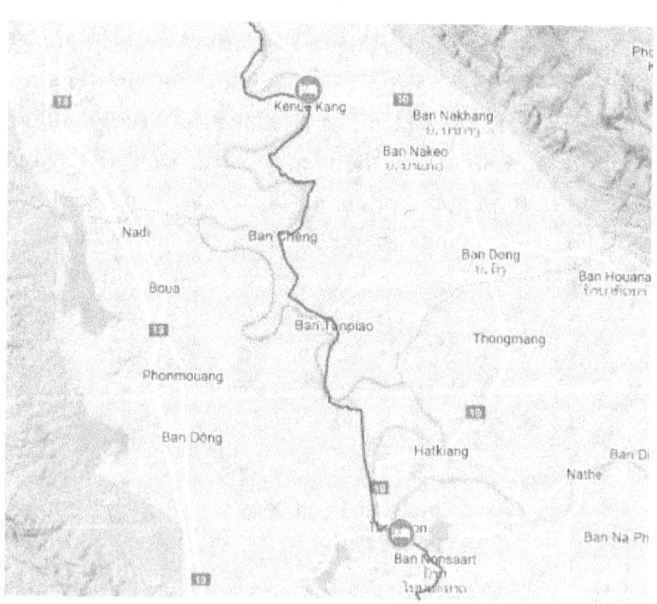

Riding the dusty backroads of Central Laos

For the next couple of days, we followed the Nam Ngum river. This took us through some idyllic, peaceful countryside and it was good to be away from the busier area around Vientiane and the border. Most of the riding was on unsealed roads. This use of, often euphemistically named, unsealed roads had concerned me before I decided to come on the trip. I had done a similar trip in Southern Laos with Chris a few years previously and the only section of sealed road I could remember was about 100 metres in length. We had spent most of our time bouncing painfully along impacted mud tracks, which separated the fields, and I had not enjoyed the experience at all. But the roads here were much better. For the most part they consisted of graded gravel and sand and were quite pleasant to ride on. We were on our way to a restaurant on the river for a lunch stop. On arrival however it turned out that because of Chinese New Year the restaurant was closed. We rode a little further in the ever-increasing heat and found another place where we gorged ourselves on delicious noodle soup and boiled eggs.

After lunch and a short doze, in whatever shade I could find, it was time to pedal, pedal, pedal again to another dusty village. This one boasted a wildlife centre, The Wildlife Refuge Centre run by the Lao Conservation Trust for Wildlife (LCTF) which was the reason it had been added to the itinerary. Of course, this time, there was no air-conditioning and we wandered from one fenced off area to the next in the continually increasing heat and humidity. Again, all I wanted to do was lie down. I wondered if anyone would notice me crawling under the wire of the bear sanctuary and making myself comfortable in the long grass.

We left the wildlife sanctuary and, after a few more miles in the saddle, arrived at another restaurant by the river. This one was located in the village we were staying in but it was late in the day and, to enable us to eat before it got dark, we decided to stop and eat first. A feature of this particular restaurant was that a DJ played annoyingly loud music which, after some cajoling, we managed to convince the owner to turn down a bit. This is a common occurrence in much of Asia. Any family or social gathering, be it wedding, funeral or birthday, necessitates the hiring of a music system with amplifiers and speakers capable of reaching the deepest of deep bass notes, and blasting them out at volumes which must surely be detrimental to the health of anyone within a few miles. Unfortunately, after a few beers, some of our group felt they needed to wail along to any familiar song, which only encouraged the DJ to play the music even louder.

Before the DJ

I was keen to leave the restaurant early, mainly to avoid riding back to our hotel in the dark. But also now, for the added reason of escaping the racket emanating from the DJ's speakers and my fellow diners. I did have lights for my bike but, as I had not yet had the need to use them, they were secreted somewhere deep in my panniers and I knew it would only get darker as I searched for them. I rode to the hotel quickly in the descending gloom. First thing the next day I attached the lights.

A Week of Chinese New Years

Day 3 – Ban Keun to Nam Ngum Reservoir – 32km biking, elevation gain 344m

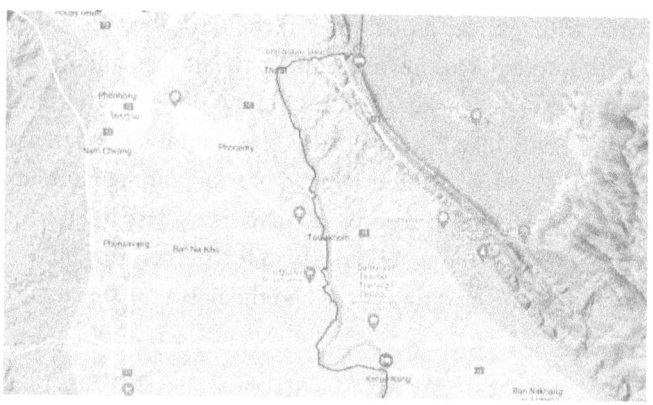

A few hills later we arrive at Nam Ngum lake

More riding, eating and, now and then, stopping to admire the view. Chinese New Year, which seems to go on for a few days, meant that the place where we were supposed to stop for lunch today was closed. We soon found somewhere else, which was probably even better, and after a huge plate of rice, pork and vegetables everybody wandered off to find a comfortable spot for a quick nap. We'd been told there were a few hills today and sure enough we encountered a number of them. I decided that I would not tackle the last, and most precipitous one, and was happy to take the truck along with everyone's baggage to the resort we were staying at. As the ancient diesel trundled up hill after hill, I was convinced my decision was the right one.

The resort was pleasant enough, with views across the lake. Dinner was the usual multi-course affair. One of the courses was the ever popular, with everyone except me, Tom Yum Soup. I entertained myself during the meal, by defining exactly which components of this sweet and sour combination one is supposed to eat.

As the resort was at an altitude of around 500 metres it became quite cool once the sun dropped. While it was good to have a respite from the heat of the day, I had not really packed for any cold weather. I did have a multi-purpose sarong, borrowed from my wife. This had come in useful both on the plane and on the trains, where a blanket was too heavy, but some kind of protection for the air-conditioning was useful. I wrapped myself in the sarong and made my way down to join the others in the bar. For some reason they found my appearance hilarious and, when one of them lent me a tea cosy hat, my ridicule was complete.

What's so funny?

A Boat, A Train, A Massage

Day 4 – Nam Ngum Reservoir to Vang Vieng – 30km by boat, 24km biking, elevation gain 179m

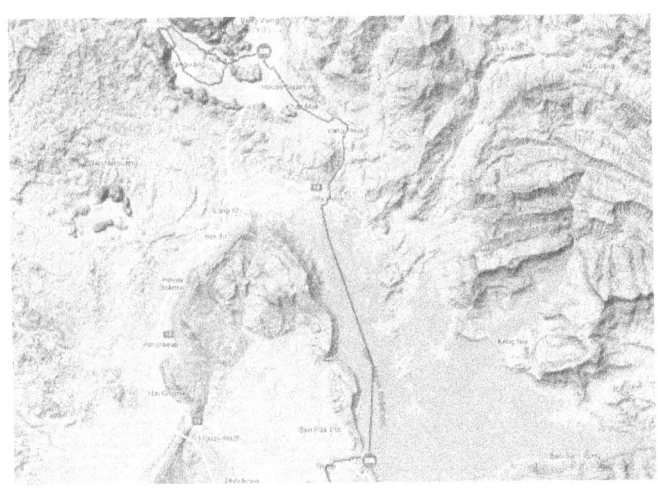

We cross the lake and strike out for Vang Vieng

We had a 2-hour boat trip today, so I was careful not to drink too much tea or coffee assuming, correctly as it turned out, that there would be limited toilet facilities on board.

Before we headed down the hill towards the lake, a large, jovial fellow with a couple of fingers missing turned up on the most dilapidated looking motorbike I had ever seen. This was the boat captain who had come to collect our bags. His stripped-down bike had a metal tray contraption attached. He grabbed our bags two or three at a time in his giant hands and hurled them into the carrier. Then he waved and shot off down the hill shouting "follow, follow." We made our way carefully down the muddy track to the small docking platform and awaited the arrival of our transportation.

Baggage handlers and boat captain

The boat crossing of the lake was uneventful and very relaxing. The lake is actually The Nam Ngum Reservoir, created when a hydropower dam was built. It now generates more than 70% of Laos' electricity. The lake was full of small islands, some of which were for sale.

En route the ever-affable captain asked if we needed the toilet as the crossing time was a couple of hours. There was a toilet on board but it was situated behind the engine and would have involved a life-threatening journey to reach it. He stopped at one of the many small islands shouting "toilet island here". The ladies who needed to relieve themselves went first, finding some minimal privacy behind a few small bushes. Then it was the men's turn. I took advantage of this small detour, managed to find a relatively quiet spot, turned my back on the others and gazed into the distance, while nature took its course.

Is this Phi-Phi island? No, it's Pee-Pee island

We docked at our destination and unloaded the bikes, ready for more cycling. The ride away from the river was very steep and gravelly. I walked most of the way. Before we had gone more than a few hundred metres, we came across a school and The Dutchman decided he would entertain the kids for a bit by blowing his horn and pretending to be an ice cream salesman. With the children amused - we rode on. There were more hills and I took up my usual position at the rear of the pack.

The road took us under the elevated high speed train line. We would be riding on this a few days later from our destination of Vang Vieng back to Vientiane. Like many other projects in Laos this new train line has been financed by China.

. . .

In recent years, China has become one of the largest investors in Laos, particularly in infrastructure projects such as the construction of roads, bridges, and railways. These projects have helped to improve connectivity within Laos and between Laos and China, which has facilitated trade and investment between the two countries.

China is a major source of tourism for Laos. Chinese tourists are attracted to Laos' natural beauty and cultural heritage, and their spending has helped to boost the local economy. With the new train line major population areas in China are now directly connected to Laos.

Overall, China's influence on Laos' economic growth has been significant, particularly in the areas of investment, trade, tourism, and aid. However, this relationship has also raised concerns about debt sustainability, environmental impacts, and social implications of China's involvement in Laos' development.

Keen to do my bit for the local economy, I went for a massage in Vang Vieng. I was interested to know what the difference was between a Lao massage and a Thai massage. I'd had plenty of Thai massages so the comparison was easy to make. I soon realised that while, in Thailand elbows are frequently used to apply pressure on certain points, in Laos it tends to be the thumbs which serve this function. I enjoyed the massage and felt invigorated afterwards.

We had dinner in a restaurant recommended by Chris, which had food from all parts of the world. I chose the falafel to remind myself of the time I spent on a kibbutz in Israel. It was excellent. So excellent that, the following evening, I had the same meal again.

One falafel, two falafel

After dinner, Areeya came with me to the pharmacy. I had developed a number of unpleasant, itchy spots on my head and face, due I think, to the sweat produced from cycling non-stop for hours. Over the previous few days, I had convinced myself that I that I'd contracted shingles, or something worse. The friendly pharmacist had a quick look at my head and then produced numerous unguents, pills and a special shampoo which I gladly purchased. Total cost around 150,000 Lao Kip, about A$12.00. And all with no prescription.

To Ride or Not to Ride

Day 5 – Visiting around Vang Vieng –
34km biking, elevation gain 287m

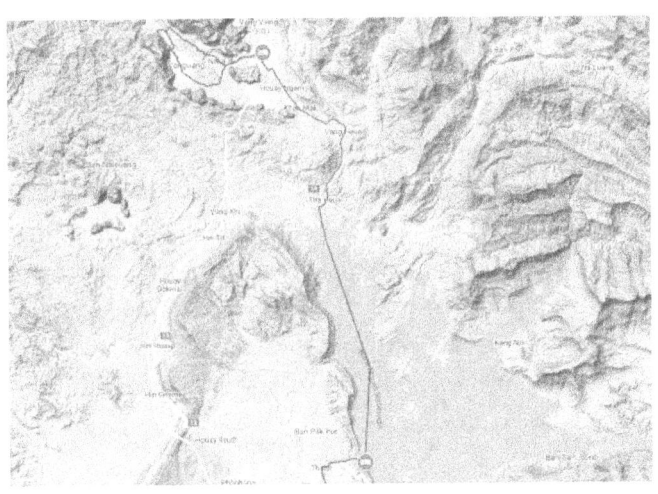

Back on dry land we take a tour around Vang Vieng

I wasn't sure about today. The plan was a 34-kilometre trip around the beautiful hills west of Vang Vieng. But I knew the roads would be bumpy and dusty and considered not joining the others at all and just hanging out in town. Then Chris suggested I join them for the first part of the day, an easy 12-kilometre ride to Blue Lagoon number two, or was it three? There were any number of them. So, I relented and we all rode off, out of town. We crossed a few dilapidated bridges and, after no more than a few minutes, were riding on the hard, rocky, spikey tracks that pass for roads around these parts. But it was a nice day, no wind and pleasantly cool. I adopted my position at the rear of the pack and pedalled along happily.

On arrival at the lagoon, the first activity was a climb to a lookout. Only 100 metres. But it was actually 110 metres at an average angle of 45 degrees and less than halfway to the top I had had enough. I turned round to begin the descent, soon realising, as I should have done earlier, that with a dodgy knee or two, down is harder and more painful than up. I'd packed an elasticated knee support, specifically for such activities, but of course, it was lying on my bed at the hotel. I took my time and made it to ground level without incident.

Uncle Fred also soon decided he'd had enough fun for one day. He descended a few minutes later and joined me watching people leaping from a platform, suspended about 20 metres in the air, into the lagoon below. We chatted for a while until I decided to investigate the contents of a nearby ice cream fridge. My resolve to avoid Magnums was fast disappearing, along with a similar plan to drink less beer, and the shiny packaging of the Magnums convinced me that I needed one. There was some confusion over the price and I paid 65,000 kip. I later converted this to about A$5.00 which seemed extravagant but was really no more than the cost of a cappuccino back home.

Once everyone else had descended from the lookout spot, and told me what I had missed, we remounted our bikes and continued on our way. As we reached the main road I knew I had a decision to make. Turn left and head back into town alone, or turn right and stay with the others. It had been a pleasant morning so far, despite the knee crunching climb and overpriced confectionary. Not wanting to appear too antisocial, I allowed myself to be persuaded to continue with the others and not to stick to my original plan of returning to Vang Vieng. This proved to be an error of judgement on my part.

We rode for 15 kilometres or so along an ever-bumpier road to another lagoon which, apart from being called, inventively, lagoon three, was exactly the same as the first one we had visited, lagoon two. I idly wondered where lagoon one might be. As a few of the group made their way to yet another lookout point, the rest of us sat quietly by the lagoon watching the antics of the, mostly Chinese, visitors. After an hour or so of this dubious entertainment we continued on our loop back towards town. It was on this stage of the journey that I fully realised my folly. The road became less and less enjoyable to ride on. The surface consisted of soft, shale like gravel, liberally scattered with large rocks. I rode on, I had little choice. Eventually I made it back to the hotel for a well needed shower, and beer.

Later that day we strolled through the night market before dinner. Those familiar with my previous books would know that I am not a fan of markets and avoid them whenever I can. Traders were selling all the normal stuff, clothes that would not fit and would look old after one wash and heaps of other useless tat. Often, in my experience, items in markets are more expensive than in an actual shop. Serendipity proved this point when, as we emerged from the market, I spotted a shop selling T-shirts and other clothing items. I went in and, after a few minutes perusing the well stocked racks, found a couple of shirts I liked. These had been available in the madness of the market but at a much higher price.

A Day to Myself

*Day 6 – Visiting around Vang Vieng –
High speed train to Vientiane, no
biking*

Today, everybody else went off to kayak along the Song river, followed by a float through a cave on an inflated inner tube. I was never going to do this, water sports are not for me, and while I realised it marked me as an unadventurous old fuddy-duddy, I was happy with my decision. I spent the morning taking a leisurely stroll through town. Vang Vieng reminded me of Kathmandu in the 70s. The hippies had been replaced by millennials and gen zedders, most sporting tattoos and all carrying mobile phones, but the general vibe was much the same. There were coffee shops and food stalls everywhere. By 10:00am I'd had three cups of coffee, two banana pancakes and a pain au raisin. Obviously, I'd picked the wrong week to lose any weight. Vang Vieng was a very laid-back place. I imagined it would get much busier once the Chinese groups started arriving but, this week being Chinese New Year, they were mostly staying at home. It was easy enough for them to get here; just a train or two across China to Boten and then a short trip on the high-speed line which ran from the China - Laos border to Vientiane and passed through Vang Vieng.

There were quite a few Israelis in town too. This explained the availability of the delicious falafel I'd had for dinner the previous night. Israelis are always easy to pick out as soon as they talk as everything seems to come from the back of their throat. This phenomenon of young Israelis being found in large numbers around the world stems, for the most part, from the country's military service requirements. Most Israelis are required to serve in the Israeli Defence Forces for a period of two to three years. After their service, many young Israelis take advantage of their newfound freedom and travel before they start college or enter the workforce.

In the afternoon I met the rest of the gang at a small river-jetty on the edge of town. My fellow adventurers floated towards me on their kayaks in the slow-moving water. I was momentarily tinged with regret for not having joined them. But it was a fleeting moment and I soon realised that, with a life full of regrets, this one would not add much to the tally. I'd had an enjoyable time in town, wandering aimlessly and observing life on the streets. The coffee and pain au raisin stop was also good. They mocked me slightly for not having joined them but I had enjoyed my day and did not feel I had missed out in any way.

On the Train

In the afternoon we rode the three kilometres to the station to take the high-speed train from Vang Vieng to Vientiane. The bikes had to be transported by truck as they could not go on the train. It had taken us four days to bike from the outskirts of Vientiane to Vang Vieng. It only took one hour to get back.

The station is massively over engineered and obviously built for future expansion. Signage on the outside is in Lao and Chinese only. Once inside we found seating for about 1000 people even though, at present, only four trains a day pass through. Trains run from Boten on the Chinese border through Luang Prabang, Vang Vieng and on to Vientiane. Accessing the station required showing a passport and ticket plus security checks. It was much like boarding a plane and not at all the easy-going train experience in most of Europe. All luggage had to be X- rayed. We had an hour or so to wait and were not allowed on the platform until a few minutes before the train departed.

There were a few vending machines for drinks and snacks but few other facilities. The main source of entertainment was to be found in the toilets, which boasted both Western and Asian style options in the cubicles. The hand-driers were the most advanced I had ever seen with numerous options for hot and cold air.

A few minutes before the train arrived, we were allowed onto the platform. Here, we were herded into lines corresponding to the train door we had to use according to our seat numbers. If anyone dared step out of line, a loud whistle was blown by one of the many security guards.

Once we boarded, I found the train comfortable and not too overly air-conditioned. There was plenty of legroom. The track is dead straight, carving through hills and across lakes and towns. Apart from leaving the station, where I guess it has to re-join the main line, there are absolutely no turns at all and, looking forward, I could see right down the length of the train at all times. All information messages were given first in Lao, then Chinese and finally English. They were all repeated three times which seemed excessive.

We were informed, as we approached Vientiane, that we would have to show our ticket at the exit or pay again. This, of course, was really no more than a ruse to make more money as the train did not stop between Vang Vieng and Vientiane and it was impossible to board without a ticket. I was concerned there would be a hold up when we exited but it was actually well organised. There were no automatic machines to cause confusion but, instead, a number of Lao girls and boys - they all looked about 16, with QR readers, efficiently checking everyone's tickets.

From the station we took a bus into town. The driver was talking on the phone most of the way, apart from the odd break to spit out of the window. I was glad my own window was closed as I was sitting only two rows behind the flamboyantly expectorating driver. We arrived at the bus station, and after a short walk through potholed streets, checked in to a small hotel in a quiet part of town.

Promenade, Passaggiare, Spaziergang

That evening we made our way to the promenade for dinner. This picturesque walkway had been built over the last few years. I recalled a previous visit to Vientiane, back in 2007 when I had first arrived in Bangkok and was keen to explore the surrounding area and nearby countries. At that time this Esplanade had been under construction so I was interested in seeing the finished article. It was a bit of a walk from our hotel to the Esplanade and on the way, we passed through a night market with a Lao food exhibition. This caused some delay as various members of our group broke away to sample the delights on offer. There were other distractions as well.

Hello, Good Evening and Welcome

We finally arrived at the chosen restaurant. At first glance I thought it was a rather pretentious place. When I discovered it was run by a French, or possibly Belgian, guy my first impressions were confirmed. There was a short debate as to whether we should sit outside in the heat, which afforded a view across the river, or inside in air-conditioned comfort. Fortunately, as far as I was concerned anyway, there were people smoking outside so the consensus was to sit inside. The restaurant seemed expensive after what we had been paying for food and drinks in the countryside. But this was the big city and the owner was French, or Belgian. As we dined, I was forced to admit the food was fabulous, even though it took a long time to arrive.

After dinner, not keen to face another long walk through the dimly lit streets, I decided to go back to the hotel by tuk-tuk. We careened through the dark streets with the driver sounding an odd, whistle like, horn at every intersection. He seemed to have no lights on his vehicle and I'm sure it was only firing on one cylinder. Not that I had any idea how many cylinders his dilapidated vehicle should have, but I'm pretty sure it should have been at least two. The short journey cost 60,000 Lao Kip, about A$5.00, for a trip of no more than two kilometres. I became embroiled in a short, but heated, discussion with Uncle Fred about what constitutes a rip off and what is a simple market rate fluctuation. My opinion was that, as I was sure a local would have said no more than A2.00 or A$3.00 for the trip, we were being ripped off. He held the view that we could afford it and therefore the driver was just exercising his skill at negotiating, what he saw as, a fair price for foreigners.

Around Vientiane

Day 7 – Vientiane to Nong Khai and on to Bangkok – 25kms biking, elevation gain 129m

Around Vientiane 67

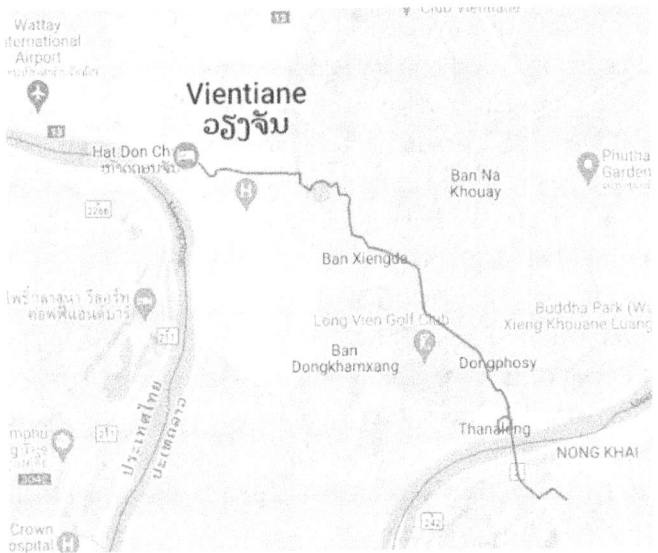

To the Thai border and beyond

Today was our last day in Laos. We planned to head off later that day to cross the border back into Thailand. We'd be taking the train to Bangkok at 6:50pm and it was about an hour's ride to the border. After breakfast we did a bit of sightseeing, on our bikes, around Vientiane, Laos' sleepy capital.

Riding a bike around any Asian capital city, probably many capital cities that are not designed to be ridden around, and especially as a group, involves some risk. But the traffic in Vientiane was light and the other road users surprisingly unaggressive. Whenever we signalled our intention to cut across in front of them to take a last-minute turn, they generally slowed down to let us go. This would never happen in Europe or Australia where a stream of invective would be hollered, along with a lengthy blast of the horn. Perhaps there were stiff penalties for knocking foreigners off their bike here? We visited the National Museum and Victory monument. Our first stop was the That Luang stupa – the symbol of Laos. A stupa is a dome-shaped building, usually a Buddhist shrine. This one can be found in all government logos and on all Lao banknotes. The stupa was originally built in 1566 when the capital was moved from Luang Prabang to Vientiane. It was destroyed and rebuilt several times before the most recent renovation in 1953. It was a quiet place to reflect, but after 20 minutes or so I was happy to take a seat in the shade and wonder if it was too early to go in search of ice-cream.

Our next stop was Patuxai, Gate of Victory, known as Vientiane's Arc de Triomphe. It was built when the US supplied cement and funds for a new airport. The Laotian government built Patuxai instead and so its nickname is the "vertical runway". Patuxai is dedicated to those who fought for the independence of Laos from France. It used to be possible to climb to the top to get a good view of the surrounding traffic. But, since COVID, that option is no longer available. I posed for a picture in front of the fountain, got wet and forgot to hold in my stomach, which due to the vast quantities of food and beer I had been consuming on this trip, was getting more and more noticeable.

Our last stop was at the Cooperative Orthotic and Prosthetic Enterprise (COPE). Between 1964 and 1973

Around Vientiane

the US army dropped over two million tons of ordnance on Laos, making it the most heavily bombed country per capita in history. Of the more than 270 million sub-munitions, 80 million failed to explode. They now maim or kill about 300 people per year in Laos. Since the war ended in 1973, more than 20,000 people have been killed or injured – half the victims are children as they are more likely to pick up and play with the bomblets. At COPE we learnt more about this horrible legacy of war. We had lunch at a restaurant owned and managed by the charity. The staff are all from underprivileged families and the charity trains them to work in hospitality. Everyone was wonderfully attentive and helpful, if not particularly efficient.

Back Over the Border

After lunch we packed our panniers and checked out of our hotel, ready to head to the border. It was a fairly easy 18-kilometre ride through a few backstreets and then onto a smooth wide road which, with a few turns took us to the Friendship Bridge and Laos/Thai border. Chris seemed keen to get to the border, so we didn't make any stops along the way. Apart from when a truck, inconvenient for everyone but convenient for me, had to stop in the middle of the road when turning. This allowed me a few seconds to grab my water bottle and slake the thirst which had been building up. I was wary of a recurrence of the *infected salivary gland, left side*, I picked up on a previous visit to Bangkok, especially with all the dust and fumes I had been inhaling on this trip.

We soon moved off again and after another 20 minutes arrived at the border. It wasn't as chaotic as when we left Thailand and an almost friendly Lao official stamped us out of his country. I think we'd timed it well as it was about 2:30 pm: he'd had lunch and a nap and was ready to do a bit of work before knocking off at 4:00pm, when the border closed. After a bit more pointless form filling, we were stamped into Thailand and pedalled off over the bridge.

As there had been on the previous crossing, there was a separate and protected walkway on the bridge which was impossible to access with bikes and was again blocked halfway across. So, we had no choice but to ride on the road along with trucks and cars. Crossing from Laos to Thailand the train tracks for the train which runs from Thailand over the bridge and into Laos were more of a hazard. Leaving Thailand, we had crossed the tracks, riding over them with no issue. On this traverse, on the far side of the bridge, as we entered Thailand, due to the angle of the track as it crossed the road, Chris got his rear wheel caught and came off his bike. Luckily there were no major injuries but he and Areeya were shaken.

Dinner Choices

At Nong Khai station, we had to arrange for our bikes to be carried on an earlier train than the one we were booked on, as ours had no cargo carriage. After leaving our bikes and bags at the station we bumbled about a bit deciding what to do for dinner.

There were a few options. Uncle Fred and his partner, who had spent three days in Nong Khai before the trip, recommended a restaurant in town on the river. It sounded nice, but time had marched on and we really only had about 90 minutes to get to the restaurant, order food, eat it and return to the station. With a large group it often takes a while to place food orders. Especially if there is anyone fussy in the cohort. We wandered across the road, to where there were a couple of not very appetising looking places and then decided we should go into town. This involved some haggling with taxi drivers who, as it often the way with taxi drivers, instead of charging a sensible price and making some money would rather state a ridiculous one, and make nothing. Even with a couple of locals among us to discuss prices in Thai, they still wanted too much and we decided to just walk the short distance from the station to the main road where there were a few food stalls. The avarice driven taxi drivers followed us a little way and dropped their price slightly but we did not succumb.

We soon found a perfectly good phad thai stand. Someone asked if they made noodle soup. Well, no because it's a phad thai stand. They do phad thai. I attempted to order for myself while everyone else listed their litany of requirements; vegetarian, no pork, no onion etc. I thought I'd successfully ordered a chicken phad thai but when I asked Areeya to confirm this with the mask clad cook, she said I hadn't ordered anything. It turned out they had no chicken or pork, just vegetarian phad thai. Well, it was late in the day. So, it was vegetarian phad thais all round.

After dinner, a few of us went to 7 Eleven. I wanted to buy a sim card for my phone. Chris helped with negotiations for the numerous and complicated deals available, while I contemplated buying a cheap pair of headphones, so that I could listen to a couple of podcasts on the train. Eventually I decided against it as I knew I already have far too many of these devices. We walked back to the station, passing the taxi drivers, and boarded our train. It was one of the newer Thai State Rail trains and very comfortable. This was when I made the discovery that if the curtain of the top bunk is closed it blocks the lights which shine all night. I remembered this was why on the trip north as I hardly slept at all. Before boarding, I depressed myself by standing on the same weighing machine as I had before we started the trip.

This revealed that I had gained five kilos.

OMG!

To Cargo or Not to Cargo, This is the Station

After a pleasant night on the train the fun began. As previously mentioned, the bikes were on another train as ours had no cargo facility. However, both trains still went to the same station. And this is where the system failed, as the new station had no functioning cargo office yet. Cargo still had to be collected from the older, Bang Sue station across the road. This, at first, sounded simple enough. But, as we discovered but you couldn't just go and pick up your cargo. It had to be taken by truck from the new station to the old one. We were told this would take two hours.

The two stations were only a couple of hundred metres apart. But there was no easy way to walk from one station to the other. You had to cross six lanes of traffic and negotiate the tracks at the old station. We accepted this challenge. It was early morning and traffic was reasonably light so crossing the six lanes was fairly easy. Access to, and traverse of, the tracks at the old station was more of a challenge. Being hit by a train was always a possibility but the hardest part of this was getting onto the tracks in the first place. There was no easy access point, for safety reasons I assumed. Eventually we spotted a rickety wooden staircase which permitted entry and we scurried across the tracks and onto the platform.

We hung around for a while at the cargo office, but there was little happening. Eventually a few of us took a taxi back to Hidden Holiday House, Chris and Areeya's place, while Chris and those who were staying in Bangkok, or going elsewhere, waited for the bikes.

Part Three

Quiet Days at HHH

Contemplation

I'd enjoyed the trip, but I was equally happy to be off the bike and enjoying the river views at HHH, as everybody called it. Pretty much everything I owned had gone into the washing machine on arrival but luckily, I'd been given a new cycling shirt by Areeya, so I had something to wear.

It was time to relax and contemplate the highs and lows of the previous six days. Certainly, one of the upsides was the weather. We'd enjoyed cool mornings and relatively mild days with temperatures between 15 and 25 degrees Celsius. Cool enough to need a light jacket or just tough it out in the morning. During the day the temperature would get up to the mid-20s most days. Still pleasant enough. Although I'd found cycling in the afternoon heat a challenge on some days I knew it was nothing compared to what I would be facing on the next trip in eastern Thailand. Additionally, on this trip, there had been a slightly different crowd than previously and it was always fun meeting new people.

One of the members of our group of cycling adventurers was an enigmatic chap, let's call him Veggie Guy. He'd been everywhere, mostly travelling alone by bicycle. I was keen to find out more about his exploration of the Indian sub-continent; he'd ridden from Lhasa to Kathmandu as well as across the border from New Delhi to Kathmandu. But he was difficult to engage with, preferring to keep to himself. So, even though I felt we may have enjoyed trading tales of the Tibetan plateau and our mutual adventures on Freak Street, Kathmandu and in Pahrganj, Delhi, it never happened.

Temples and Markets

I had a quiet day as planned. Got up around 06:30am and went for a leisurely bike ride, on my own, around the local area. There's a temple, there's always a temple, a few kilometres away and I rode there for some contemplation by the river. Back to HHH for a massive breakfast of eggs, bacon, tomato, two slices of bread and jam and some fruit, got to have something healthy. I returned to my room to read and relax. I went out again around 10:00am for another short ride to Huay Phlu, the local town. I appreciated the freedom of riding alone and at my own pace and schedule. In Huay Phlu I visited the new temple, I told you there's always a temple, which judging by the gaudy statues around it, seemed to have something to do with animalism and the King of clubs. I should probably have tried to investigate further but, there are so many temples scattered around Thailand. Trying to understand why they are all there would take a lifetime.

. . .

Temples and Markets

After lunch I dozed and read again until around 3:00pm when Chris asked if I'd like to accompany him to the market to pick up dinner for us and some other guests who had just arrived. As I was eating so much, any opportunity for exercise was welcome. We set off and I managed to keep up for about a kilometre but then, knowing the way to our destination, I let Chris, who I knew was making a valiant attempt to keep his pace down, go on ahead.

I really hate markets. We parked our bikes and plunged into the maelstrom. We were in search of fish, green curry, a duck dish of some kind, vegetables, mango and sticky rice plus some other accompaniments. I also, sometimes, hate being six feet tall; usually this dislike of my otherwise useful stature, only sets in on planes with minimal legroom but Asian markets are another location where my *vendaphobia* combines with relative gigantism. Racing from stall to stall, trying to keep up with Chris, who was more familiar with the locale than I, I had to constantly remember to bend low or else be strangled by the twine and string which kept the umbrellas aloft.

When I wasn't avoiding a casual garrotting, I was ducking my head, which needed no further injury, to avoid colliding with an ill-placed metal strut. All of this combined with the increased heat produced from the various gas burners and open fires used to cook and heat the food on offer. It's probably mentioned somewhere as a level in Dante's Inferno.

. . .

Purchases completed; Chris suggested we visit the other new market which had just opened. Things were much calmer there with wide aisles and stalls that were way over my height. It was all very organised, though I guess a bit sterile. Chris informed me that the new market opened everyday whereas the old one is only twice a week. People, being averse to change, preferred the old market so when it was open, it was always the busier of the two.

We rode home, getting caught behind a large local on a small scooter. He was wearing a T-shirt with the word *Volunteer* emblazoned on it. I decided, somewhat cruelly, that he must volunteer to eat all the food that was left over from the market. The street we were riding on was narrow and there was no opportunity to pass the rotund recalcitrant, who was oblivious to the tailback behind him; cars, a truck or two, and a Polish/Canadian and British/Australian cyclist. Eventually Chris saw an opportunity to accelerate and exerted extra pressure on his pedals to zip past the obese obstruction. I risked doing the same, the cars couldn't follow us as there was no room. As I passed the lumbering lad, fully expecting him to be chatting, or watching a movie on his phone, I was surprised to see that no, he was just not in a hurry. I admired his attitude and lack of guilt, wishing I could emulate his equanimity and lack of concern for those he was inconveniencing in such situations.

Temples and Markets

We arrived back at HHH with our bags full of food and I retired to my room to shower, relax, and after a few minutes, to eat again.

The other guests turned out to be a friendly, older Dutch couple. They came from a town called Vlissingen. I attempted to add to the conversation by pointing out that, when I was younger there was a ferry service from Sheerness in Kent, to Vlissingen. I only used it once as it took much longer than the Dover or Folkstone ferries which plied the channel. But, joining the conversation was a challenge. The husband-and-wife couple, who had obviously been a couple for a long time, had their own peculiar conversation style. She would talk at length on a certain subject, finally taking a breath towards the end of an anecdote. He would then add a couple of words to finish it off.

For example:

Her - *We are from a small town in the south-west of the country, between Antwerp and Rotterdam. It's a port city but you would not have heard of it.*

Him - *It's called Vlissingen.*

Me - *Yes, I took a ferry from England there once.*

But they had already moved on to another subject.

I had a similar experience one New Year's Eve at a friend's place. I've never been a great conversationalist, but I like to think I have some skills in the area. I do at least understand that listening is an important factor. Not everybody does. I was introduced to a chap who hailed from North London. I think it was felt that, as a London native myself, we would have something in common, if only an accent, and would enjoy reminiscing about the city of our respective births, while making full use of glottal stops, juxtaposing our final w with a v sound and saying fink instead of think (the dental fricative). I don't do any of these, but it's common when speaking in a London accent, innit?

But, that's not how it went. He asked questions, not with any real interest in the answer, but as bait for his own revelations on how amazing his life had been. At some stage he discovered I had lived in France for a while:

- *whereabouts?* he asked

and when I replied

- *in the south, the Nice area*, thinking he might enquire further about my favourite restaurant, or if I had learnt much of the language, he simply informed me:

- *I stayed at the Negresco hotel there.*

This experience reminded me of a time when I returned from riding a tandem across Europe, fully detailed in *My Brother's Bicycle*.

- *Oh*, said a friend, *I went to a new disco last week.*

Well, it was the 70s.

When it comes to a lack of interest in conversations, I'm as guilty as the next person in certain situations I suppose. If the subject turns to sport, I just switch off, gaze into the distance and wait for a more interesting topic to come along. It seldom does.

Living Next Door to Alice

The next morning, one of the neighbours was having a housewarming party. This required loud, but fortunately quite tuneful, with minimal overbearing bass, music to be played from just before dawn. I was told it would usually start at 05:00am, an auspicious time of some kind, but we were lucky as the cacophony did not erupt until around 05:45am. It was impossible to sleep and I read for a bit before rising and heading out for a short ride to, you guessed it, another temple close by. This one had some kind of Chinese influence and consisted of a number of Confucius style, gargoyle characters surrounding a central building. There was also what appeared, to me at least, to be some kind of space tower in the centre, possibly used to contact deceased relatives. A little further from the main complex was a large gate, which looked out across the river, and had a set-up of some pleasant-sounding wind chimes. I wandered around taking pictures before returning to HHH for breakfast. I stuffed myself with pancakes, bread and too much coffee. I passed on the fruit and fresh coconut.

Music was still pumping from the neighbour's place; it would go on all day. The fact that I found it annoying doesn't mean I do not like, or appreciate music. *Au contraire*, on both bike trips I made sure I had a small speaker attached to my handlebars, so that I could select suitably inspiring songs to help me pedal with even more enthusiasm.

What it does mean is that I have a sense of taste. Despite this, I have listened to some awful stuff too. Mainly due to a job I had in London in the early 80s, where I was employed as a ticket agent for a theatre agency. Apart from giving me pretty much free access to shows at West End theatres, this role also allowed me to pick up seats for the various musical acts playing around the city. Unfortunately, as it was the 80s, I witnessed some execrable musical talents; such as Kid Creole and the Coconuts, The Thompson Twins; there were three of them, hilarious, and Simple Minds; Scotland's answer to U2. However, I did, on the other end of the talent spectrum also see such class acts as Jackson Browne, Warren Zevon and James Taylor. All of these I saw twice thus, almost cancelling out the evenings I sat listening to lesser talents, wishing it would soon be over.

Just before I left the agency and moved on to more gainful employment, and with the company struggling to make ends meet, they decided to pay us, on Christmas Eve, knowing banks were already closed and would not reopen again for a few days, by cheque. Cheques we were unable to cash. Normally salaries would be deposited direct to our bank account but this subterfuge gave them a few days, during which, I assume accountants and management sat in darkened rooms thinking of ways to save the company.

So incensed was I by this act of financial trickery that, a few weeks later, when a friend asked me to buy 18 tickets for an Eric Clapton concert at Hammersmith Odeon, I took his cheque, got the tickets but did not pay the cheque into the company's account. I got no financial benefit from this myself but felt I had, in my own small way, paid back my Scrooge-like employer for their deceit.

Part Four

Quiet Days In Bangkok

Inane Conversations with Taxi Drivers - An Avoidance Strategy

My taxi ride back to Bangkok was uneventful. After a previous close scrape, due to my tendency towards urinary incontinence, I'd ensured I did not drink any beverages before leaving. The driver, a friendly chap, was only around 5ft 0 but he had his seat set well back, and his arms gripped the steering wheel like steel rods, as we careened along the main road into town. But he knew where he was going, wasn't constantly on the phone and I had my seatbelt tightly fastened. This is a relatively new feature for back seat passengers of Thai taxis. Previously, assuming no self-respecting Buddhist, firm in their belief of a preordained fate and reincarnation, would imagine that even a relatively minor accident could affect them. So, drivers would deliberately hide the rear seatbelts under the seat making it impossible to wear them. The only solution to this life-threatening act, which I often used, was to sit in the front seat next to the driver. This did mean you were a few feet closer to whatever jingly-jangly music or, worse still, English Football Association match he might be listening to while he drove, and occasionally chatted on his phone. But at least you could wear a seatbelt.

When I lived and worked in Bangkok, I developed a useful strategy to avoid pointless conversations with taxi drivers taking me to the office. Because our building was located close to the US embassy, it was always assumed that I was American. Now and then, especially if I was tired or a bit hungover, I'd just say *Yes*, anything for a quiet life. But mostly, I'd reply *No*, depending on my mood, *England* or sometimes just to spice it up, *Australian*. I soon learned that England was a mistake as the driver would immediately start naming league football teams. Leicester City, at the time, was owned by a Thai Billionaire. For some bizarre reason most driver's team of choice was Wolverhampton Wanderers. There was some entertainment value in this as they would pronounce the name in their own unique way. I tried to be friendly but after the first dozen or so times of simply naming football teams I had heard of, just to play the game, as it were, I could take no more. When I said I was Australian at least the conversation was brief, usually just consisting of a short, but animated exchange of:

Taxi guy - *Crocodile Dundee.*

Me - *Yes, him.*

Taxi guy – *Kangaroo.*

Me – *Yes, kangaroo.*

After a while I came up with the brilliant strategy of declaring myself Canadian. I worked with a chap from Canada and he put me on to this subterfuge. Most drivers knew little or nothing about this wonderful country; neither ice-hockey nor Leonard Cohen were popular in Thailand, and after mulling over what they could add to any cultural exchange, would usually fall silent and go back to listening to Wolverhampton Wanderers play Manchester City - another favourite team.

Don't Believe the Reviews

We arrived safely in Bangkok and the driver found my hotel with no problem and even drove a little way down the short, narrow alley leading to it. I was staying in a part of town I wasn't familiar with. When planning the trip, knowing I had 10 days to amuse myself between the two bike trips, I'd contemplated a few options to fill the time. One of these was a trip to Prachuap Kiri Khan, a beachside town a few hours south of Bangkok which I had visited a few times. But ultimately, I'd decided just to explore a new area of the city itself and, searching through various hotel booking sites, I'd come across the small hotel where I was now headed. Reviews were mostly good and it sounded interesting. The hotel was located in Thonburi. An older part of Bangkok which I, wrongly it turned out, assumed would be chock full of interesting places to explore.

The taxi had dropped me a short distance from the entrance, as the road was blocked by a small black Volkswagen with a D for Deutschland tag on it. I took my bags from the boot and walked the last few metres to the accommodation. There was a middle-aged woman sitting outside smoking, but she didn't look Thai and made no attempt to acknowledge me or communicate. I wandered into the hotel where a young girl was sweeping the floor. She ignored me too, more out of shyness than anything else, I'm sure. There was a small desk which I assumed was reception, but no-one was sitting there, or anywhere near it. The lady who had been wafting smoke outside, wandered in and spoke to me in German. We had a little chat, in German, about options for entry and she left me to work things out for myself. If my stay here in this odd little corner of Bangkok achieved nothing else, at least I would have had my ego stroked by the opportunity of using one of my limited language skills. I assumed she owned the car but I had no idea what her connection might be. Perhaps I would find out later, assuming she survived the night, as she did not look too well and all the smoking at her age must surely be having an effect. I was glad I finally gave it up for good at age 34, about 20 years too late.

The downstairs area of the bizarrely named, *J No 14* hotel, was filled with strange artefacts; stuffed animals, old motorbikes and kid's toys from the 1950s and 60s. I tried to converse with the shy girl in English and then, using my limited Thai, but to no avail. We had reached an impasse as she continued her sweeping and I waited, assuming somebody would emerge from the crepuscular surroundings to check me in. After a few minutes of nonaction, I spotted a small stand on the desk with a key and a piece of paper. Further investigation revealed my name and arrival details, along with a room key. I picked it up and said to the shy girl, knowing she would not understand:

- can I take this and go to my room?

This goaded her into action and she rang someone, whom I assumed was the owner. The shy girl handed me the phone and after a brief, but stilted, conversation with the owner and then her daughter, who spoke better English, I was told,

- no problem, the maid will take you to your room.

I handed the phone back to the shy girl who spoke briefly into it before putting down her broom and heading up a flight of stairs. I dutifully followed.

At first glance, the room reflected the ambiance of the downstairs reception area, but maybe it would grow on me. Enticingly, there was a small desk and chair in one corner and I imagined myself as Henry Miller in his garret in Paris, manically typing out the first draft of Tropic of Cancer.

I am living at the Villa Borghese. There is not a crumb of dirt anywhere, nor a chair misplaced. We are all alone here and we are dead.

. . .

I unpacked a few things. Not much, as I was already thinking I might change my plan to spend three nights in this odd place. Just a couple of shirts and some underwear. After a bit of trial and error, I worked out the lighting activation and air-con system. The switch for the bathroom light was well hidden but I eventually located it.

After a short rest to recover from the check in experience and an investigation of the room facilities; the bed squeaked as I had known it would, I wandered out in search of food and drink. I waited until 5:00pm as I was aware that 7 Eleven, the ubiquitous purveyor of beer, snacks and other sundry items, due to Thailand's arcane licensing laws, would only unlock their fridges at 5:00pm. They also did this between 11:00am and 2:00pm for lunchtime drinkers, or those who can plan ahead. It was a fairly pointless deterrent really as you could get a drink in a bar at pretty much anytime and, if you could find a mom-and-pop store, which you usually could, they'd sell you booze whenever they were open.

Before going out, I had checked on Google for the location of the nearest 7 Eleven. There were two very close; 200 metres and 210 metres in opposing directions. Logically I chose the closer of the two. On arrival all was good and I wandered around in the air-conditioned, well laid out store, picking up a few other items I needed. The beverage fridges were lined up against a back wall and I searched in vain for the one containing beer, to no avail. It occurred to me that this 7 Eleven may be Muslim owned or franchised as most of the ladies on the tills were wearing headscarves. I took my other purchases to the counter and bought them anyway employing my language skills to ask if the 7 Eleven sold beer.

- *Mi beer mai - do you have beer?*

- *No alcohol,* said the be-scarfed young
    lady in perfect English,

- *go to another store.*

Ah, the one that is 210 metres away from where I'm staying. I'll know next time. As I left, I was pleased to see they did sell condoms, not that they were on my shopping list, so maybe they had their priorities right and at least were not Catholic owned.

I retraced my steps, passing the lane which led to my hotel, and completed my shopping at the other store. Back in my room I gorged on my favourite Thai snacks, and the beer that I told my wife I wouldn't buy. Maybe I should have taken the hint at the first 7 Eleven? No alcohol.

Later in the evening the owners turned up. The mother and daughter I had talked to on the phone earlier. When I asked about places to eat in the area, they kindly offered to drive me to the local mall in their Mercedes. How could I refuse? We squeezed down the alley and turned left towards a corner of a busy road where they dropped me off. I found the mall with no problem but, after a short investigatory walk around, decided I would rather eat at a Japanese place I had spotted earlier. I retraced my steps but was unable to find it. Back in my room I decided to skip dinner, I didn't have much choice, and just have an early night.

A little later I understood why the previous occupant had unplugged the noisy fridge. I was about to do the same, when I remembered I had bought two yoghurts which needed eating before I could deactivate, and therefore silence, the fridge. When I'd bought the yoghurts earlier, on an impulse, I'd told the seller that I didn't need the plastic spoons they always insisted on providing. I'd done this more out of habit than anything, not realising that I no longer lived in Bangkok and in an apartment with a fully stocked kitchen. Also, because *mai ao choon* - literally, don't want spoon, was one of the phrases I had mastered in Thai. It along with *mai ao thung* – don't want bag, came in handy and helped in some small way to save the planet. Without it any purchase, no matter how small, at 7, would always be placed in a plastic bag. If it was a food item of some kind, appropriate cutlery would also be provided. I'm all for a bit of customer service but, assuming you have it at home, who really needs a plastic spoon, wrapped in plastic along with a single yoghurt, in a plastic bag. Buy two yoghurts and you'd get two spoons. I think they've stopped dishing out plastic bags now and you have to pay for them but the plastic cutlery is still provided, unless you refuse it.

But, on this occasion, doing my bit to save the planet turned out to be a mistake as I had no other cutlery. So, there I was, nakedly slurping yoghurt with my fingers before unplugging the fridge. Such class.

Early Check Out

The hotel I'd booked on a whim, in an attempt to explore an area of the city I was unfamiliar with, turned out to be a bit of a disaster. The owner/managers were friendly but did not reside at the property and there were no onsite staff apart from the previously mentioned, uncommunicative maid.

My room was comfortable enough, although it lacked any real ambiance. The final straw was the fridge clunking on and off until I unplugged it.

The main attraction of the place seemed to be the owner's penchant for collecting stuffed animals, skeletal remains and other artefacts. Or, as any sane person might describe it, crap. I mooched around the next morning waiting for a breakfast that never arrived, despite a colourful sign which proclaimed – *Breakfast from 8 am* – and took a few pictures of the paraphernalia that festooned the downstairs area.

There was no sign of the owners, the shy girl or the German smoking lady, by 08.30 am so I left some cash on a desk in the foyer, along with my key, and walked out of the door.

I headed in the direction of an area of the city I was familiar with. I planned to check-in to a hotel I had seen online many times, that I wanted to investigate. The BTS, one of Bangkok's mass transit systems, had been extended since my time living here and, slightly confused, I managed to board a new shuttle train going in the wrong direction which, if I had discovered its existence the night before, would have taken me to a couple of places to eat.

Changing trains and heading in the right direction this time, I was soon back around the Nana district and on Soi 8. I checked into the hotel I had selected and was happy with everything, except a clicking air-con unit. After a quick room change, I settled in. There was even a spoon for yoghurt consumption, impressive.

The area I was staying in has quite a reputation as an entertainment district. Entertainment for which Bangkok is well known. It's true that while there are plenty of places where more than food and drink are on offer, it also boasts a large number of perfectly innocent restaurants and bars. It's also very close, just a couple of stops on the BTS, from the main shopping areas of the city, so a very convenient place to stay.

To Thai or not to Thai

On an achievement high following my successful hotel switch and subsequent air-con challenge, I walked to the nearby Monsoon Cafe and Bar, one of my favourite local watering holes. My confidence level was so high that, on arrival, I engaged my waitress in a short conversation in Thai. It went something like:

Me - *Hello, how are you?*

Her - *I am fine. How are you?*

Me - *Also fine. It's a bit cold today isn't it?* (*I was quite proud of this; 2 phrases including an adverb of time and use of the question format*).

Her - *Yes, it's cold.*

That was about it. Then I studied the menu, intending to go one step further and order in Thai when she returned. My linguistic plot was foiled when a different lady appeared to take my order. She was less friendly than my original waitress. My confidence quickly dissipated and I resorted to pointing at the menu and mumbling.

Monsoon is a lovely spot, I even liked the music they were playing; light soul and country at just the right volume. I amused myself *shazamming* for a while to identify what I was listening to. I'd never heard of any of the songs or singers but I wasn't really surprised, as my musical tastes are firmly stuck in the 1970s - when all the good stuff was released.

A Walk in the Park

With Bangkok experiencing relatively cool weather, I took a long walk around the area where I used to live and back to my hotel, through the newly constructed Benjakiti park. This was developed on land that belonged to the Thai Tobacco Monopoly. They've done a great job creating a green space, which Bangkok generally lacks.

I'd often visited this area during the years I lived in Bangkok. It had always been a good place, one of the few, in fact, in the city where riding a bike was actually a pleasure and not a life-threatening experience. Until a couple of years ago the only areas for riding in the park were either the perimeter road, or a separate bike track in the, then quite small, park itself. The issue with the bike track was that tree roots had won the battle with asphalt and there were many very bumpy areas. The other challenge was coming across a happy-go-lucky local who had wandered on to the clearly marked bike track while deeply engaged in a relationship with their phone.

Since the renovation there was now a lengthy, well laid track, stretching for a few kilometres with separate, well marked cycling and walking areas. Even the walking area was marked with a lane for walkers and another for runners, although most people took little notice of this demarcation.

It was on my way home from the morning walk in Benjakati that I discovered a cannabis coffee machine.

A Walk in the Park

It's coffee Jim, but not as we know it

It was painted bright green and, for the sum of 20 baht, about A$1.00, various beverages were available, all apparently laced with cannabis. It seemed too good an opportunity to miss. In my youth I'd dabbled with cannabis, pot, dope, whatever you want to call it. But I'd always found the seriousness with which the process was completed, frustrating and ultimately, annoying. Also, usually my few drags on the finally produced joint would be taken after an evening in the pub. All that happened was I'd feel sick and want to go home. Often not realising that I was already there.

. . .

Intrigued, I slid my 20 baht note into the machine and pressed a button for a canabis (sic) coffee, then waited expectantly. The machine whirred and gurgled for a few seconds before depositing a steaming beverage behind a small perspex door. I picked it up and took a swig, continuing to consume the pleasant tasting coffee as I proceeded further along the street. It was hard to tell whether the slight feeling of euphoria I started to experience was due to the coffee itself, or what was, possibly, contained in it. My knee and back, which had been bothering me, on and off, for a few years, felt better too. But I could not really believe the Thai authorities would allow drugs to be sold from a vending machine, accessible to people of all ages. This did not stop me from returning the next day and indulging again.

The Det 5 Story

In the evening I had dinner, and a beer or two, at Det 5, another lovely spot in the shade. Det 5 is a long-established restaurant in Bangkok. It's existed for 30 years, though not in its present format. It all began at Buckskin Joe Village on Soi Zero. This street was also known as Tobacco Road because it led to the, also now defunct, Thai Tobacco Monopoly area. The bars and other dubious entertainment in this area are long gone. Like many other establishments, Det 5 started out in a wooden shack with one bar counter top and five bar stools. It was originally called Sexy Night. A different time indeed. Here's an explanation of the name from their website:

Origins of the first "Sexy Night - Det 5"
Long before cultural and economic forces prompted the homogenisation of the Bangkok night scene, one bar stood to differ from the usual uninspired and impersonal offerings.

This bar was known as "Sexy Night - Det 5" — A Unique Identity.

Whilst the "Sexy Night" moniker will have prompted instant cognition, the "Det 5" name warrants further explanation. After the Vietnam War, the United States began searching for its servicemen missing and killed in action in Southeast Asia. Operational detachments were established throughout the region to provide the command, control and logistical headquarters of the Joint Task Force known as Full Accounting or JTF-FA.

Originally located in what was then Old Buckskin Joe Village, the Sexy Night Det 5 beer bar became the unofficial, yet officially patronised "Fifth Detachment" or "Det 5" of the Joint Task Force. Cold beer, rock 'n roll jacked up to "11", and engaging personal service were the intoxicating ingredients of a bar that many came to call their "local".

Bongo, Bongo

Any time I stay in a new hotel room, or at a friend's place, I'm always initially intrigued and, soon after, annoyed, by the noises I hear and didn't expect. Last night was no different. Around midnight I was awoken but what, I swears sounded like someone playing the bongos nearby. I lay still for a few moments wondering if it wasn't just a dream, but it continued. I went into the bathroom where the sound was louder; a rhythmic pounding beat and imagined some ancient, doped up hippy, taking advantage of Thailand's lax new laws on the purchase and use of cannabis, exploring his soul through music. After a while the noise abated and I assumed he'd fallen asleep.

A few hours later I could hear the static of a radio playing some kind of news program. I wasn't sure but the language sounded like Chinese. Someone was obviously checking out for an early flight and was keen to know what was happening back home. A bit after that, I heard them clunking down the stairs with their oversized suitcases. Then, for a short time, all was quiet again until around 05:30am, when the pleasant but invasive sound of the birds started, along with the street traders setting up outside. Around 06:00am I got out of bed and made tea, ready to start my day. There was no use swimming against the tide.

I became intrigued by the bongos, which over the next few days, I heard a few times. I eventually worked out that what I was hearing was the water tank in the bathroom refilling. The gurgling of the water heard through the chipboard wall reverberated and echoed creating a rhythmic sound of African drums. The positive aspect of this experience was that I had to Google *bongos* to find out more. Here's what I discovered:

Ethnomusicologists have theorised that the origin of the word "bongo" comes from the Bantu words ngoma or mgombo, meaning drum. The bongo's earliest musical roots are found in the Eastern provinces of Cuba in the Changüi and Son, two musical genres that feature the bongo as the sole percussive drum.

Down Memory Lane

Tympanic investigations complete, I figured it was time to visit some old haunts. Back in an area of the city I was familiar with, this was easily accomplished. First, I went to the Central department store. When I had first arrived in Bangkok and people talked about *Central* it confused me. If I needed to buy something people would say, *go to Central* and I'd assume they meant the city centre.

There are any number of these stores scattered around the city, probably too many. Central Chidlom was my local branch and I had spent many a happy hour there, in the cool interior, searching out items I didn't really need to purchase. I'd never really been there on a quiet morning in the week before. I had usually visited in the evenings, or first thing on a Saturday or Sunday morning, when even though it would still not be crowded, it was quite busy. I wondered how bored the numerous staff must be, forced to listen to the constant, annoying advertising blasting out in a variety of languages; Thai, English - with a particularly grating American accent, and Chinese, on repeat every five minutes or so.

I was reminded of my own foray into the world of department store employment, when I had worked for the now defunct, chain of Debenhams in Canterbury. I earnt £36.00 a week. Not a vast sum, even in 1975. I was taken on originally as a casual Christmas extra, working, of all places, in the toy department! Can you imagine me and toys and kids? My contract was extended to cover the post-Christmas sales period and, finally, my retail skills were recognised and I was offered a permanent position. I worked there for about a year. I was bored to death most of the time - dreaming of travelling to India and desperately trying to save something for the trip from the pittance I was paid.

Today, aware that I shouldn't be drinking beer every day, I bought some wine. Thailand, or rather, its government, has a strange attitude to wine. Inspired no doubt by the fact that mainly the rich, and foreigners, drink it, it's highly taxed, unlike beer and whisky. A bottle of anything halfway decent usually costs around A$20 or A$30. You can buy a bottle of local spirits for half that amount. If you shop around and look low enough on the shelves, you can sometimes find a bargain. I picked up a bottle of something Australian for 299 baht, around A$12.00. All the cheaper wines seemed to be from Australia. I wasn't expecting much but, for a change, I wasn't disappointed. It was quite drinkable and later, during the night, meant I didn't need to get up every hour to empty my restricted capacity bladder.

Let the Train Take the Strain

The next day I had breakfast at the hotel. I'd planned to go to Det 5, which had a fairly extensive and attractive looking breakfast menu, but it didn't open before 11:00am! For a moment I thought I was back in France. So I had breakfast at the hotel. I was pretty impressed with the food on offer in the small hotel restaurant, really just a seating area with a few tables and fans just by the entrance. After being given instructions on how to use the coffee machine, I served myself a portion of fried rice with a couple of fried eggs and some surprisingly tasty, but anaemic looking, sausage. The sausage tasted strangely sweet. They also had fruit and pastries so, all in all a good offering, for 220 baht, about A$10.00.

Later I took the BTS and connected to the MRT in the direction of Sanam Chai, to visit the Thai Museum that had been suggested by Chris. Bangkok's public transport systems have expanded rapidly in the last decade or so. I remember my first few visits to the city when the only way to move around was by taxi or tuk-tuk. On one visit I distinctly remember it taking three hours to reach the city from the airport. There are two rail options depending on your destination; the BTS or the MRT. There's also a relatively new, third train link to get to the main airport, Suvarnabhumi.

Bangkok BTS stands for Bangkok Mass Transit System, also known as the Skytrain. This rapid transit system, which operates above the ground, elevated from the street level, serves as one of the main modes of public transportation in the city.

The Bangkok BTS consists of two lines: the Sukhumvit Line, and the Silom Line. The two lines intersect at Siam station, which is one of the busiest stations in the system.

The MRT, or Mass Rapid Transit, is the subway, or underground system in Bangkok. It was opened in 2004 and currently has two lines: the Blue Line and the Purple Line. When I first moved to Bangkok in 2007, the MRT did not yet have any TV screens on the trains, blaring out inane, pointless advertising and was a very calm environment in which to travel. This has changed now and ecstatic looking actors constantly share the virtues of numerous skin creams, fast food and expensive cars, among other things.

. . .

All of the transport lines are frequently extended to reach further out into the sprawling city suburbs.

The two systems connect at various points. What doesn't yet connect are the ticketing systems. Each has their own, meaning any journey involving a connection requires two tickets.

Anyone who lives in Bangkok, or, like me, visits frequently, purchases a smart pass which can be kept topped up and avoids queuing each time to buy tickets. The BTS version is called a Rabbit pass. The MRT version seems to have no similar moniker, but does have a large M emblazoned on it to avoid confusion.

After a comfortable journey on the wonderfully air-conditioned trains, I emerged from the MRT, pleased to find the museum had its own exit and did not involve a walk in the sweltering heat. The same station also serves the Grand Palace and Wat Pho, home of The Reclining Buddha, so there were plenty of other tourists disembarking. A surprising number of French people seemed to be visiting. I guess it's better than staying home and going on, or enduring, the strikes. The cold snap, with temperatures dropping below 20c overnight and struggling to reach 30c during the day was over and Bangkok had returned to its standard *too hot* status.

. . .

As I waited for the 10:00am opening hour, a gaggle of small children appeared accompanied by at least half a dozen teachers. So much for a quiet visit. But they were well behaved, the kids that is. Apart from the occasional squeal, they caused no issues. The museum was fairly uninspiring. Its main aim was to show how *Thainess* works, or what it means to be Thai.

There were a few exhibitions of clothes and typical Thai accoutrements all of which might have been interesting for a tailor but left me cold. I left after 30 minutes or so and made my way to the other place that had been recommended as a new feature of the city to visit; namely a Sky Park. This, as the name suggests, was a suspended park above the Chaophraya river. Google helped me locate the park which was pleasant enough, but very exposed and, therefore, very hot even if it afforded some lovely river views.

Dining on the Observation Deck

Later that evening, back at Det 5, I gazed around at my fellow diners and amused myself, making the following observations:

- A foreign guy sits with two girls. All three are gazing at their phones. I assume one of the ladies is his girlfriend and the other her friend, who has been invited along for the evening. He's drinking beer, but they've ordered a bottle of wine, an expensive choice in a Thai bar of any kind. The table is already straining under the weight of the food they have ordered and more is arriving all the time. They talk excitedly in Thai, as he continues looking at his phone. He doesn't speak, so I am unable to guess where he is from. I sense his desperation, and growing fear of the bill he will later pay with a begrudging smile.

Dining on the Observation Deck

- I'm waiting for my food to arrive when a guy and a young Thai girl, she looks about 15 but is probably 25, take the table next to me. The girl is glued to her phone, but he catches my eye and engages me in conversation. He has an English accent, from somewhere up north which I can't place. He soon tells me he's from a town in the Lake District. As she orders three meals and chats with her mother and friends on her phone, we continue our conversation. As many people do, he thinks I'm Australian and I do not correct him. I say conversation, but really, it's just him talking, keen to extol the virtues of his lakeside life, assuming I had never been there. He was right in that assumption at least. As his girlfriend chews her way through the numerous items she has ordered, for which he would no doubt be paying, we continue our aimless chat. He doesn't ask me where I'm from, or what I am doing in Thailand. He's also keen to divulge the various pleasures available in Bangkok. Had he asked, I would have shared with him that I lived here for eight years and am quite familiar with them.

- A little later, as I'm paying my bill, three older Danish people take up another table close by. They are speaking to the waitress in English but I can tell they are Danish straight away from their accent. When they switch to Danish, I amuse myself for a while, trying, and mostly failing, to understand their glottal stop filled conversation with its 27 different vowel sounds.

Bars of Bangkok

Today was a hot polluted day and I spent most of it inside, hoping the air-con would filter out the high level of PM2.5 particulates in the air. The forecast says no real change is expected before the weekend when the wind will pick up from the north.

On my evening venture into the sweltering heat, in search of sustenance and entertainment, I went to a bar that had been recommended. I knew on entering I had made a mistake but, before I could turn around and leave, a friendly waitress had approached and I was forced to order a beer. I took a seat and waited for the beer to arrive. I'd entered one of those establishments, you'll find them all over Bangkok, which assumes, correctly for the most part it must be admitted, that everyone wants to watch, and more annoyingly, listen to, the nasally, over-excited commentary of some obscure ball-based sport.

. . .

I drank my beer quickly, paid my bill and left in search of a better ambiance. There are bars in abundance in this area of Bangkok, the infamous Nana district and I had no problem finding one that met my needs; no sport, no annoying music. The sticky heat hung in the air. Overhead fans were trying valiantly to move it around. A fat guy in a black shirt was sitting at an adjacent table, sweating profusely. His unsightly appearance brought home to me how I must have appeared myself. So much so that I momentarily wondered if I had sat near a mirror.

When I lived in Bangkok I would always, as a minimum, wear a collared shirt, shorts and covered sandals when I went out to socialise. But now, in an attempt to minimise the effect of the heat, I've taken to wearing flip flops and a singlet when I go out in the evening, figuring I just don't care anymore. I never did this when I lived here and now wish I had. The feeling of freedom, with no sleeves sticking cloyingly to my shoulders and the air wafting between my toes, was palpable.

Shopping

The next day, in search of lightweight clothes, I went to MBK, one of Bangkok's many sprawling shopping malls. But, as I discovered on a previous visit, Tokyu, a Japanese department store that used to sell such things, was gone. I found a cheap thin singlet in a sales area downstairs and then left; there was nothing there for me anymore. In another shopping centre I came across a branch of Uniqlo, another Japanese chain store specialising in urban streetwear. I could shop in Uniqlo in Brisbane but they have different stock here. I used to avoid this store as they had a custom of shouting loudly in greeting at anyone who came near the front door but they've stopped that, so you can now approach the entrance without being hollered at. I found some wonderfully lightweight t-shirts and left happy, looking forward to wearing them.

In the evening I ventured out to Det 5 again. The food there wasn't the best, but the service was friendly and the ambiance wonderful. I sat quietly with a beer perusing the menu. A couple of Russian guys took the table next to me. They talked intensely, but I couldn't understand anything. Occasionally I picked out the name of a local store and then I heard the one Russian word I'm familiar with, *rabotti* - work. I imagine they're saying *shopping is hard work*. Not the kind of conversation I expect them to be having. Shouldn't they be discussing Putin and his disastrous invasion of Ukraine?

I took a stroll after dinner and was pleased to find a walk through the nearby, Evangelical Church of Bangkok grounds, which links up to Soi 10 and the park I like to visit. This will make my morning strolls that bit easier.

Tom's Diner

Tom, my nephew, came into town for a couple of days. He lives in Hong Kong and has a high-powered job with a bank there. I went out to the airport to meet him. The flight was early but as always, the processing took time. Keen for a coffee I went to a branch of Lawsons. This chain of snack and beverage stores exists in competition with 7 Eleven and offers much the same services. They don't serve coffee as such but you can buy a sachet and mix it with the hot water provided. I asked for the one with no sugar. But in Thailand, this just means no sugar already mixed in with the coffee, so when I fought my way into the plastic package, I found two sachets of sugar which I simply threw away.

Tom arrived and we travelled back to town on a variety of trains as I explained how the three Bangkok city rail networks, have separate ticketing systems. This is inconvenient, but no great hardship, as long as you know. I'm sure one day a politician will cleverly devise a card which covers all three methods of travel. How hard can it be?

In the evening we joined another friend for dinner at Det 5, where else? The heat continued but the restaurant didn't really have an indoor seating area, just a space inside for pool players. It was a particularly sweltering evening and I was quietly wilting, despite my new super lightweight clothing, so enjoyed frequent visits to the toilet via the air-conditioned part of the building.

Bangkok Backwards

I took Tom on my standard Bangkok tour. This normally followed a route I had come up with when I lived there to give visitors a taste of life in Thailand's capital. It usually started with a trip on the river but today, due to where I was staying, we did the trip in reverse. We started out by taking the BTS to National Stadium as Tom was keen to visit the Jim Thompson Museum.

Jim Thompson House Museum in Bangkok is a popular tourist attraction that offers a glimpse into the life of Jim Thompson, an American businessman who played a significant role in reviving Thailand's silk industry in the 1950s and 60s.

The museum is located in a traditional Thai-style house made of teak wood, surrounded by lush gardens and canals. The house was built in the 1950s by Jim

Thompson himself, and he lived there until his mysterious disappearance in Malaysia in 1967. The house was turned into a museum after his disappearance and has been open to the public ever since.

Inside the house, visitors can see an impressive collection of Southeast Asian art, including Buddhist sculptures, paintings, and ceramics. The interior of the house is beautifully decorated with a mix of Thai and Western furnishings, and the architecture reflects the influence of traditional Thai design.

The Museum also offers guided tours for visitors, which provide a deeper insight into Jim Thompson's life and his contributions to the Thai silk industry. The tours are available in multiple languages, including English, and are included in the admission fee.

I'd been there a number of times during my years living in Bangkok, but there had been a few changes in the intervening years and Tom and I spent a pleasant couple of hours there. This included a meal and a drink at a new restaurant.

Then we took the khlong ferry in the direction of Khao San road. Khlong means canal in Thai and travel on these ferries is a uniquely Thai experience. They have been made safer in recent years following a fatal accident. Hearing that there had been an accident did not come as a great surprise. Boarding and alighting used to be a perilous affair, which involved clambering through the spaces on the side of the boats that served as windows. Now the authorities had sensibly remodelled both the ferries, and the piers from which to access them, providing a much safer way to board.

Khao San Road is a small street located in the Banglamphu neighbourhood of Bangkok. It's known as a popular backpacker destination and has a colourful history. Originally, the area around Khao San Road was a rice market and a place where traders and farmers would come to sell their goods. During the 1980s, however, the area began to attract budget travellers and backpackers who were looking for affordable i.e., cheap, accommodation in Bangkok.

Over time, the area developed a reputation as a hub for those travelling on the cheap, and it became known as a place where they could find low-priced hostels, restaurants, and shops selling a variety of souvenirs and other goods. Today, Khao San Road is still popular among young travellers, although it has also become a popular tourist destination for people of all budgets and ages.

In recent years, there have been efforts to transform Khao San Road into a more upscale destination. The local government has implemented new regulations to clean up the area and improve safety, and there are plans to upgrade the infrastructure and amenities in the area.

. . .

Despite these changes, Khao San Road remains an important part of Bangkok's cultural and social fabric, and it continues to attract travellers from all over the world who are drawn to its unique atmosphere and rich history.

As we left the Khao San road area in the direction of the Chaophraya river, where I was planning to take, first a river ferry, and then the BTS back to my hotel, Tom bade me farewell and took a taxi to the airport for his flight back to Hong Kong.

On the way back to my hotel, I stopped off at BNH, a major hospital in Bangkok and a place I had visited many times for various ailments. I'd been trying to phone BNH as I was concerned that a nagging pain in my lower abdomen might be the signs of a hernia. They answered the phone once, but then I was left hanging for an eternity, while some relaxing music played. So, I took the BTS to Sala Daeng and walked to the hospital. The young doctor who I saw with minimal delay poked, prodded and squeezed before declaring, *no hernia*. He did spot that my nether regions were a little swollen and assured me this was related to posture and was muscle related. I was relieved not to have to undergo surgery.

As I was in the building, I also made a visit to the dermatology department, to confirm that the issue I had experienced in Laos with my scalp was on the mend.

Here a young woman, who surely liked to use all the available skin products herself, judging by her unblemished, but also unnatural appearance, took a cursory glance at my scalp and, with an air of diffidence, prescribed some kind of scalp cleanser. The hernia checker had done a thorough job and taken quite an interest in my medical history down below. The same could not be said for the skin lady, to whom I seemed more of an annoyance, as I did not require any kind of expensive laser treatment and only needed some cheap unguent. I paid my bill, which came to around A$100.00 for both consultations and left.

Unfortunately, when I returned home a few weeks later, the nagging pain in my groin returned and a visit to another doctor, followed by an ultrasound, revealed that I did indeed have a hernia, undoubtedly obtained on those bumpy roads in Laos.

Spicy, Funny

That evening, I tried a new place nearby for dinner with the unusual name of 8855. I tried to investigate the derivation of this name but found nothing, as the establishment is quite new. So, I came up with my own theory. In Thai, the number 8 is *bphet* and the number 5 is *haa*. *Bphet* is very similar to *phet* which means spicy. *Haa* of course, is the sound you make when you laugh. So, *spicy, spicy, haa, haa*. This may be completely wrong and there are various complications caused by the tone rules of the Thai language, which I'm not even going to try and explain, because I can't. But it's good enough for me.

The food was excellent and the service friendly but the ambiance, and the air, was spoiled by a guy outside smoking a reeking cigar. Quite why, in this day and age, anybody considers this socially acceptable behaviour is beyond me.

. . .

After a short walk the next morning, I decided to investigate the breakfast options at 8855. I wasn't sure what time it would open, but on arrival at around 08:30am, things were already happening. I later discovered it opens at 08:00am, very sensible. As on my previous visit the night before, I was impressed with the food and the service. Unfortunately, for some reason, this place seemed to attract every smoker in town. Or maybe today was national smoking day? There was a small balcony where smoking was allowed. It was rightly banned inside any buildings many years ago. One guy next to me, asked if he could smoke inside and was shyly, but firmly, told by the staff that he had to go on the balcony/terrace to indulge in his habit. Extra points to the staff on this one. So, slightly distanced from coughing expats, I enjoyed a cooked breakfast and a tasty latte.

That same evening, I went back to 8855 again for an early dinner. All went well, until the cigar smoking idiot turned up and again assailed us all with his pungent fumes. I left as soon as I could. But not before muttering *tosser* under my breath and coughing loudly in his direction. He ignored me of course. I guess people with strange, annoying, anti-social habits, are used to being disparaged in such a way and simply become inured to it.

Burger King, Hungry Jack's

A day or so later, figuring I'd be eating mostly Thai food on the upcoming bike trip, I went for lunch at Burger King. Apart from satisfying the urge we all have from time to time for a juicy burger, I also fulfilled another need here. I had been looking for hand sanitiser to replace the small bottle I had brought with me from Australia, which was almost empty. But I couldn't find it anywhere. Supermarkets and pharmacies only sold large, half-litre bottles, which I did not need. Most shops had a bottle on the counter as you entered, as did Burger King. So, while waiting for my order, I surreptitiously filled my bottle from the large container on the counter. Necessity is the mother of invention.

As I ate my lunch, two Thai ladies sat at a table nearby and had a loud conversation. I have numerous theories as to why many people all over the world feel the need to talk so loudly. I think in Thailand the need to shout almost all the time comes from living in villages where families often buy a large block of land. Then they build two or three houses, one for each family and, instead of walking in the heat to have a conversation, they simply bellow across the fields to each other.

After a while, I realised the music this establishment had decided to assail its patrons with, was annoying me less. Then I realised, for a short time at least, it was because I could hear instruments being played and not just some repetitive, programmed noise. After a short respite, a nasally female began wailing over an electronic, thunking sound and things were back to normal. It was hard to decide what was more annoying; the caterwauling females or the shrieking singing.

That evening I tried another new place for dinner, called Buddy's Bar. There's a small chain of them scattered around the city. It's Swedish owned apparently, but definitely American themed. I intended to have a beer and eat there too, as they offered various types of European sausage.

But I didn't stay long. One of the few other patrons was an annoying American guy, seated just one table away, talking bloatedly about how wonderful he and his life were. In addition, another fellow, who I think was Irish, it was difficult to be certain as his excited phone conversation was almost indecipherable. Due to the volume it was being conducted at however, the entire bar, if not all of Bangkok were privy to it. The music was annoying as usual, but bearable as it wasn't too loud. Some kind of monotonous beat with flaccid lyrics. I enjoyed my Guinness and returned to the sanctity of my room.

Part Five

Bike Trip 2 - Eastern Thailand

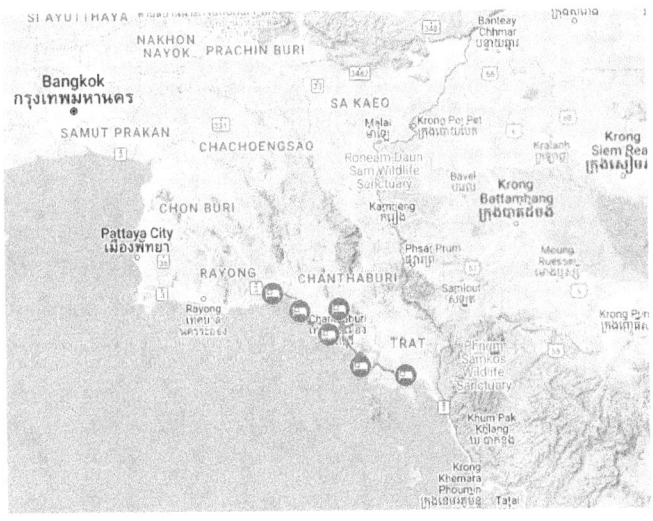

Map showing areas visited in this region

On the Road Again

Day 1 – Travel day to Ban Pak Nam Prasae – 8km biking, elevation gain 30m

The crew picked me up in Bangkok and we drove to Pak Nam Prasae in the east of the country. About four hours drive. The taxi driver was pretty good but he, as all Thai taxi drivers seem to do, spent vast amounts of time on his phone. He was wearing earphones and for the most part it probably didn't adversely affect his driving too much. But now and then, usually as we approached a junction or traffic light, he would pick up the phone and gaze at the screen for a while. When he wasn't doing that, he would spin a little device on the steering wheel to alleviate his boredom. Now and then, he would react to another road user. At least he wasn't watching a video.

· · ·

We checked-in to our guesthouse in the village. Pak Nam Prasae is located on the east bank of the Prasae River. There are many well preserved old wooden houses here. Some of them have been turned into homestays, others into restaurants and one, a small museum with pictures showing the village in the olden days. We biked to the nearby beach where the HTMS - His Thai Majesty's Ship - Prasae frigate is located. Originally commissioned in 1944 as the USS Gallup (PF-47) she joined the Pacific war zone in the same year and then the Korean War in 1950. She was also loaned to the Soviet Navy in anticipation that the Soviet Union would join the war against Japan in 1945 for four years. She was transferred to the Royal Thai Navy in 1951 and was used until she was decommissioned in 2000 and turned into a museum ship. We had lunch at one of the several small restaurants close by.

After lunch, instead of a nap, which would have been my preference, we were back on our bikes again to pedal off to the Golden Meadow mangroves. These mangroves are a vital part of the ecosystem in the area, providing habitats for various species of plants and animals. The mangroves are a popular tourist attraction and are often explored by boat. Visitors can witness the natural beauty of the mangroves and observe the diverse wildlife that inhabits the area, including various species of birds, fish, and crustaceans. They also provide an important ecological service, such as protecting the coastline from erosion and storm surges, filtering pollutants, and storing carbon. However, like many mangrove forests around the world, the Golden Meadow mangroves are threatened by human activities such as logging, aquaculture, and tourism.

Our arrival coincided with a large group of Thai tourists and we became the attraction, fielding many questions and being photographed. It was unusual for foreigners to come to this part of Thailand and we were, for a short time at least, quite a novelty. Once through the melee at the entrance, some of us rode, while others walked, along a narrow, raised boardwalk through the mangroves. The walkway continued for two kilometres and the further we went the more dilapidated it became. Soon, all of us were walking and pushing our bikes to avoid the high risk of plunging into the murky depths of the brackish water below. The path was maintained, but as most people did not venture more than a few hundred metres along it, most of the maintenance was done on the first section. Leaving only foolhardy foreigners to explore the last, less safe, part. We arrived triumphant at the exit just as the Thai tourists were piling back into their air-conditioned bus. As we waved their friendly faces goodbye, I was touched by a tinge of envy, not to also be travelling in such style and comfort.

Our next destination was a shrine honouring Somdet Kromluang Chumphon. Somdet Kromluang Chumphon, also known as Prince Chumphon or Father of the Thai Navy, was a member of the Thai royal family and a renowned military leader. He played a key role in the development of the modern Thai Navy and is widely

On the Road Again

respected for his contributions to the country's military and maritime history.

Prince Chumphon was born in 1880 as the son of King Chulalongkorn (Rama V) and Queen Savang Vadhana. He received his education in Thailand and later studied abroad in England, where he gained knowledge and experience in maritime and naval affairs.

After returning to Thailand, Prince Chumphon was appointed as the head of the Royal Pages Corps and later as the Commander-in-Chief of the Royal Thai Navy. He played a key role in modernizing the Thai Navy, introducing new technologies and strategies that helped the country to better defend its coastal waters.

Prince Chumphon was also involved in a number of military campaigns during his career, including the Franco-Siamese War and World War I. He was widely respected for his bravery and tactical skills, and his contributions to the Thai military continue to be celebrated to this day.

In addition to his military career, Prince Chumphon was also known for his philanthropic work, particularly in the areas of healthcare and education. He founded a number of hospitals and schools throughout Thailand, and his legacy continues to be felt in the country's healthcare and educational systems.

. . .

Prince Chumphon passed away in 1923 at the age of 43, but his contributions to Thailand's military, maritime, and social development continue to be remembered and celebrated today.

History and geography lessons over, we finally returned to our guesthouse. I had enjoyed the day, but it afforded me nowhere near as much pleasure as the shower I had once back in my room, followed by a cold beer, in air-conditioned comfort.

The riding, or more, my ability to enjoy it, so far had been OK. Either I had suddenly become super fit or, and this is much more likely, the pace had decreased. Most of the other people on this trip were about my age so maybe Chris was keeping the pace slow. The big difference between this trip in Thailand and the previous one in Laos was that it was ridiculously hot, every day, all the time. Most days the mercury, or whatever they use in weather apps these days, climbed to 30 degrees by early morning, peaking at 32 or 33 degrees by early afternoon. And it was humid, really humid. Cycling in such conditions meant that, although I spent most of my time on the move panting like a dog, at least the breeze created by motion helped. But, when I stopped, especially in any unshaded area, the sweat just poured off. I'd pedal drippingly along, devising more and more imaginative ways I could attach a shower of some kind to the handlebars of my bike.

More Meandering in the Mangroves

Day 2 – Ban Pak Nam Prasae to Laem Sadet – 31km biking, elevation gain 180m

The morning started with a short ride to another mangrove area after which we arrived at a secluded bay on the water. This was to be our breakfast stop and also boasted, a little further around the bay, a fish farm of some kind. Our breakfast entertainment was provided by the fish, which had a habit of squirting water great distances. The amusement value of this did not last too long for me but some of the group found it hilarious. Then we moved on to an area which contained the fish farming demonstration. This was an exposed area of netted zones of various sizes and I decided, along with another member of the troupe, Manu to stay in the shade. We found some very comfy chairs and, after a short conversation in French, were happy to quietly relax while the others wandered in the heat, looking at fish. My concern was growing that the heat would continue to increase as the day progressed, and we still had around 30 kilometres of cycling to complete.

As predicted, the heat continued to rise. As we rode along, I found myself longing to stop every time we passed one of the ubiquitous 7 Elevens. Imagine my joy when, as the sun approached its zenith, I rounded a corner and saw that Chris, who was always at the front, had pulled over in front of one of the biggest 7 Eleven shops I had ever seen. I pulled up alongside him and, while I took off my helmet and sweat soaked gloves, tried to imagine the bliss I was about to experience.

Walking through the store's sliding doors was surely like entering paradise. The gaggle of young staff greeted me with the customary, *sawadee ka, chern ka* - hello, welcome. Stores are always arranged in the same way, with aisles full of snacks and other useful, or semi-useful items and a row of refrigerators lined up against the walls. I made for one of the refrigerators, grabbing a 500 ml bottle of my favourite beverage, a corn flavoured Lipton's ice tea, along with a litre bottle of cold water. Then I made a beeline for the confectionary area, selecting not one, but two Beng-Beng bars. This was a local favourite I had discovered a few years ago. It originates in Indonesia. All the western choices were also available; Kit-Kat, Hersheys, etc., but only at inflated prices. The Beng-Beng costs five baht, around 20 cents.

. . .

Another wonderful feature of this particular store was that it had a small seating area with tables, so you could enjoy your purchases in air-conditioned comfort. I took advantage of this feature joyfully, gazing through the window at the scorched landscape outside. A sense of foreboding developed as I swallowed my refreshing corn flavoured tea and chewed on my Beng-Beng. Foreboding brought on by the knowledge that soon, I would have no option but to, once again, enter the steaming vision of hell beyond the glass.

My View on Philosophy

Other people on the trip seemed to have mistakenly decided that I have a negative attitude towards life. Of course, I know this is not the case and that I am, as Henry also often claimed, *The Happiest Man Alive*. Having opinions about certain situations and being able to see how they could be improved does not, in my book at least, mean that I am negative.

For example - when we entered the 7 Eleven to buy some items, there were four staff on duty. One of them was making a drink for someone. Another was busy counting some items. One was wandering around with a phone doing some kind of stocktake. Only one seemed to have been given the role of actually serving customers, but she was a bit distracted. When I dared mention this situation, I was immediately accused of being a glass half empty sort of person. I've noted before that this is not negative at all, as a half empty glass can be filled, whereas a half full glass implies you have consumed half of the contents and do not require a refill.

Half full or half empty?

I was reminded of the wonderful comment of my late, lamented friend Mike Preston, ironically one of the most opinionated people I ever knew, who would say:

- I often find it best not to have an opinion.

In essence, just keep it all to yourself. Don't try and make constructive comments as you'll just be accused of all sorts of negativity. Sure, everything is wonderful. As Voltaire said:

- We live in the best of all possible worlds

On the subject of philosophy, this is as good a time as any to clarify one of my other favourite sayings. This one from French existentialist, Jean-Paul Sartre, namely:

- *L'enfer, c'est les autres* - Hell is other people.

I'm as guilty as anyone else for taking this to simply mean that the worst thing you can encounter, is other people with all their annoying habits; talking loudly on public transport, reclining their seat on a plane, kicking, or swinging on the back, of my seat on a plane. Pretty much just being on a plane with other people is Hell indeed.

But that is not the meaning that Jean-Paul intended. The line, which comes from his play, *No Exit*, implies that it is other people's observation of an act that causes the issue. For example, drop an item on the kitchen floor, pick it up and eat it. No problem, if no-one sees you do it. But, as George Costanza in Seinfeld, discovered, when he tucked in to a barely touched cake he had extracted from the garbage, if you're observed doing it, you are judged a disgusting, filthy beast.

With the day's ride over, we checked into our hotel. It seemed nice although, as always, there was a duvet on the bed and no sheet. Madness in this heat. I removed the duvet from its cover, intending to use it lie on and the fitted sheet as a cover. The aircon seemed to work but the room was quite large and the aircon was struggling to keep it cool. This may explain why it was set to

19 degrees Celsius when I switched it on. I had no option but to leave the aircon on when I went out for dinner.

But, before we could have dinner, Chris had another expedition planned. We set out, in the supposed cool of the evening, to walk to a lookout point. This was described in the information we received before the trip as; *a 2.2km long walk which climbs a small hill.* About halfway to the top, as we trudged along in the still sticky heat, we came upon a statue of some kind with a small car park. I naively thought this was our goal and, after admiring the view for a moment or two, and getting my breath back, was ready to head back to town for a relaxing dinner and cold beer. I was ready to do this anyway, despite being told there was a bit further to go. I didn't want to be antisocial, so allowed myself to be cajoled into continuing the trek. Manu, sensibly turned back. When we reached the final summit, we were rewarded with great views at the Noen Nang Phaya Viewpoint. Although I didn't really think they were much different to the view we had had at the previous stopping point, a sweaty kilometre or so previously.

But the torture wasn't over yet. From here we walked another 500 metres, on the flat this time, at least, to the tip of the Kung Wiman peninsula. There, another short walk along a rocky pier, took us to the Chedi Klang Nam - Chedi in the middle of water. The chedi was built to protect the fishermen when heading out from the bay into open ocean waters. This walk to the end of the pier did afford a fabulous view of the Kung Krabaen Bay, which we would be visiting the next day.

Finally, a few of us took a motorbike taxi back to town while the others walked. I was surprised anyone wanted to walk back but apparently there was a shortcut!

Tackling the Hills

*Day 3 – Laem Sadet to Ao Yang – 45km
biking, elevation gain 286m*

The next day we were faced with some small hills. Each of us had a different approach to this challenge. A couple of people rode up them as if they weren't there. This was not the case for me and certainly not for Manu. I'd say this was the time when Manu and I bonded at a new level. I'd already enjoyed practising my French with him. I decided to do this as he always told me he couldn't understand me when I spoke English. I found this odd, as he seemed to have no problem with Chris or my wife, Tracy both of whom have their individual accents: Chris being Canadian and Tracy Australian. So, I'd taken the opportunity to have the occasional chat with him in his native language which I think he appreciated. If he didn't, at least it was good for my ego.

. . .

These occasional chats reminded me of two other people who had joined previous trips. They were also French and friends of Manu. Unfortunately, due to health issues they had been unable to join us this time. I'd spoken French with them now and then but also, as one of them was German language teacher, enjoyed the chance to use my German.

Gems and Beer

*Day 4 – Ao Yang to Chanthaburi – 30km
biking, elevation gain 150m*

The next day, a relatively short day's ride brought us to the town of Chantaburi. Famous for its gem market. The plan was to visit the gem market in the early evening as we had many other places to see before that.

The first item on our packed itinerary for the day, was a visit to the Khao Laem Sing Forest Park where there was an old fortification called Pom Phairi Phinat, built during the reign of King Rama III to guard the entrance of the river. The fort sits on a small hill and the trip was to continue up the hill to the Laem Singh lighthouse and then to Ao Krathing beach park. I say was to, because I decided to skip these, no doubt fascinating, places and to instead, do some washing and enjoy the comfort of an air-conditioned room, in what was surely the best hotel in town.

I arranged to meet the others later, to cross the bridge over the Chanthaburi river and go to Laem Sing town where we visited two places of interest. The first was simply called Tuek Daeng - Red Building. It was the site of the Phikhat Patchamit Fort, built in the reign of King Rama III. It was subsequently turned into living quarters and military command post by the French army. A single story, red-tiled roof building, today it serves as the Laem Sing district public library. There was a fair bit of construction work going on there but the builders seemed happy for us to wander around among their pointy tools and the gaping holes in the floor. I could not imagine this being allowed back home in Australia where, even when the council was changing a light bulb somewhere, roads would be blocked off and warning signs placed everywhere. The other place of interest was the notorious Khuk Khi Kai - Chicken Shit Jail, which was built to hold Thais who resisted the French occupation of Chanthaburi in 1893. A seven metre high, square-shaped prison, it was built with bricks with each side measuring 4.40 metres. The walls had holes for ventilation. The porous roof is said to have been used as chicken coop, giving the prison its name. Manu seemed particularly affected by this sad period of his country's imperial past.

Next was an 11-kilometre ride to the Chanthaburi Grand Canyon. This, now abandoned, earth and gravel mine was filled with water and, together with the adjacent boulders and hills, produced some beautiful scenery although it's not quite as impressive in scale as the name would imply.

After another four kilometres we arrived at the village of Nong Bua, which was known for its weekend, Thai Dessert Market. Here we walked around among the well-preserved wooden houses and some interesting street art. In the market we had the opportunity to sample such delicacies as Monkey Wiener and Buffalo Muff. I can only assume the names lost, or more likely, gained something in translation.

Finally, riding another 11 kilometres brought us back to Chanthaburi town, the provincial capital. Records indicate that the areas of Chanthaburi and Trat have been known for their rubies and sapphires extracted from nearby mines since the 15th century. It was not until the 1962 coup d'état in Burma, when the military nationalized the gem mines, that Chanthaburi became the Ruby Capital of the World, famous for the exceptional Siamese Ruby. The ruby mines were mostly depleted by the turn of the century, but Chanthaburi evolved from a gem mining area, to the biggest gem trading and cutting centre in south-east Asia. While most of the gem dealers have offices in Bangkok the cutting and treatment is done in Chanthaburi.

. . .

As the day progressed and the temperature dropped a little below 30 degrees we walked to the gem market. I wasn't impressed, but then I didn't expect to be. What do I know, or care, about gems? The market seemed to consist of lots of, invariably fat, Indian guys sitting around looking bored, all with piles of gems for sale. I expect there may be more to it than that. After 10 minutes or so, I'd had enough of the crowds and the heat and set out to walk back to the hotel intending to get a beer on the way. But all I found were shops selling various types of gem related grinding and cleaning equipment. There were a few trendy looking cafes and I suppose if I had gone inside, they may well have sold beer as well, but it wasn't obvious.

Back at the hotel, after the obligatory shower, I took a nap in the air-con. Later, in search of refreshment before dinner, I checked the location of the nearest 7 Eleven. This was, according to Google, the vast distance of 450 metres away. That may not sound far but, when I was living in Bangkok there were three 7s, as the locals call them, no more than 100 metres from my apartment. The reason for the local version of the name as 7 is that people can read the 7, which is shown as a number, but not the Eleven part, which some marketing genius has decided should be shown as a word. I'm sure this works well in English speaking countries, and in those that do not use a different alphabet. I set off to make the hike to 7 but on the way I came across another small shop selling just what I wanted. I bought two bottles of Leo, which was fast becoming my favourite Thai beer. Not only is it slightly cheaper than the alternatives, it's also so much easier to drink. I successfully eschewed the offer of a plastic bag from the friendly harridan who served me and also understood my request for two bottles of Leo - how fluent I have become? It's only taken eight years or so.

Back in my hotel room my problems began. I had no bottle opener. So, necessity being the mother of invention, I tried a few tricks I'd seen other desperate drinkers use. My first attempt was to try to open one bottle by clipping the two caps together and, supporting one with my fingers, prise open the other. I failed miserably. Next, I attempted to use the small space between the door hinge and the wall as a sort of vice. This released the cap a little, but all that happened was a mass of beer spray shot out of the bottle, all over my shirt and glasses. I finally tried to use my nail clippers. I failed dismally again, only succeeding in slicing open the skin on the knuckle of my forefinger. Blood poured out at quite a rate before I applied a band-aid.

Then I had a brainwave. This brainwave should have been to have packed a bottle opener in the first place. Temporarily defeated, but now in even more need of alcohol, I ventured down to reception, sure that they would be able to supply the needed equipment. As I left my room, I happened upon a friendly foreign guy, sitting quietly in a comfy chair in the corridor, smoking. He was sensibly drinking beer from a can. When I commented that I was on my way to reception to find an opener, he offered to assist, and in less than a second, had opened my recalcitrant bottle with the edge of what looked like a cigarette lighter. Feeling this was not the time to decry his addiction to smoking, I thanked him profusely and returned to my room to enjoy a now somewhat flat beer. At least it was still cold.

The plan for dinner that evening was to visit the night market. However, I was hopeful that Areeya would persuade Chris to go to a restaurant. I understand that when he is on his own, it's fun for him to wander around the market, chatting to the friendly locals and eating whatever takes his fancy. But as I may have mentioned, I really don't like markets.

The Fast Route to Paradise

*Day 5 – Pilgrimage to Khao Kitchakut –
no biking*

On the itinerary the next day was a trip to a sacred mountain. Things started well enough with a 30-minute drive in an old, but perfectly roadworthy van. I scored the front seat and enjoyed the ride out of town. Our driver, who for some reason was wearing not one, but two pairs of glasses, dropped us at a market and temple complex a few kilometres out of town. As we walked through the temple grounds, over amplified monks were blessing anyone in sight. We wandered through the market, occasionally sampling various foods. Then we arrived at a large open area where we picked up another truck, which would take us the eight kilometres up the mountain. After this, a further kilometre or so had to be done on foot. We piled into the back of a powerful diesel and prepared for the ascent. There were no seatbelts so we all braced ourselves against anything solid we could find.

The driver floored the accelerator of his vehicle and approached the first kilometre or so with gusto. The road was well maintained, but had some steep hills and sharp bends. Our driver seemed keen to prove his manhood and took these bends at breakneck speed. Soon, I began to feel slightly nauseous, as did a couple of other people. We stopped at some kind of official entrance and a few of us spent five minutes debating whether or not to carry on. Walking the rest of the way was discussed, but the idea soon abandoned, as there was something close to seven kilometres to go and the path was very steep and muddy. Eventually the driver was cajoled into driving more slowly. As it turned out, the rest of the path was really too steep and too muddy to go at any great pace anyway and it seemed that he had just gone a bit crazy on the first section.

On arrival at the top, there was a quagmire of a car park and, guess what, another small shrine with monks intoning sacred texts. We began the ascent to the top of the hill on foot where, apparently, there was a Buddha footprint. The climb was on a slippery stone track. As we began the first stage of the ascent, I could feel my breakfast beginning to come alive. That, combined with the prospect of climbing hundreds of steps, on a hot sticky day, with hundreds of other potential pilgrims, made me realise at the first stopping spot, that I really did not need to do this. I returned to the car park and said I would wait for the others there. After availing myself of the dubious toilet facilities, I toyed with the idea of beginning the climb again but decided against it. I would have been quite happy just to sit quietly and wait but this was a challenge due to the constant stream of loud safety announcements. I noted with interest that there was a first aid office and an ambulance available. Further shattering of the peace was made by a guy managing the pickup trucks with a loud hailer. So much for quiet contemplation. Eventually, I found a relatively peaceful area, where I could amuse myself listening to a couple of podcasts. Unfortunately, this was quite close to the toilet where I had recently relieved myself and there was quite an unpleasant odour wafting my way. The time passed slowly.

An hour later the rest of my group slowly reappeared. They didn't look much enlightened and I guessed that, despite their efforts, they had not achieved Nirvana yet. After a few minutes for a group photo in the mud and smoke, the smoke caused by the numerous candles and incense, lit by those seeking paradise, we boarded another truck to make the descent. I was a bit nervous about this, assuming the driver, aided by gravity would speed down the dangerous gradient. After all, I was told, they were paid by the number of trips they completed, so for them, the faster the better. But the return driver was a much calmer fellow and the trip down was quite pleasant. We thanked him profusely for his safe driving as we left his cab.

A Trip to Chanthaburi Cathedral

Back at ground level, we found our duo-bespectacled driver waiting to ferry us back to town where we picked up our bikes and the fun continued. We still had the cathedral and art gallery to mooch around in the heat. The irony of a Thai town called Chanthaburi having a cathedral was not lost on me. Near to my home town in Kent, stood the imposing Canterbury Cathedral, which I had been forced to visit on many occasions. Inside the cathedral was at least cool and we strolled through its sanctified pews.

Quite why there's a cathedral in the middle of a town in Thailand, a mainly Buddhist country, is a story in itself. Apparently, it was built by Vietnamese refugees. Chanthaburi Catholic Cathedral, also known as the Cathedral of the Immaculate Conception. The cathedral was built in 1711, and has undergone several renovations over the years. It is a beautiful example of European architecture, with elements of French and Italian design. The interior

A Trip to Chanthaburi Cathedral

of the cathedral is also quite impressive, with intricate stained-glass windows, ornate altars, and a stunning ceiling. The Chanthaburi Catholic Cathedral is an important religious site for the Catholic community in Thailand, and attracts many visitors each year.

Our scrapes with religion complete, we finally made our way to a small art gallery near the cathedral. This was in fact just a house which a local artist, while still living there, had turned into a gallery to display his own paintings. After a short visit, as we crossed a bridge back to town and, who should we meet but the artist himself, working and selling his wares, on an adjacent street.

The Man Who Didn't Love Islands

*Day 6 – Chanthaburi to Ko Jik Island –
56km biking, elevation gain 280m*

We had over 50 kilometres to ride today. Our destination was a small island in the Welu River estuary called Ko Jik. Chris loved finding out-of-the way places like this. I'd have been happy with another night in Chanthaburi, which was slowly revealing its charms. The previous evening, not being overly keen to eat at the market, I'd gone to a small restaurant in town on my own before meeting the others. The owner was a lovely, friendly lady who spoke good English. She seemed genuinely happy to see me when I pitched up just after 5:00pm. I ordered a beer and some spaghetti with sausage which was lovingly prepared. I enjoyed this, admiring the view across the river. Around 6:00pm I had made my way back to the hotel to meet the others and we'd headed off to the market. Actually, the market was pretty good; not too crowded and, whilst you could wander around looking at, and ordering, any interesting food, there was also the option of sitting at a table and ordering from a menu. I wasn't planning to eat, as I had already had my spaghetti, but an interesting looking waffle took my fancy. Later, I also ended up consuming half a plate of phad thai and another half a plate of fried rice, which my colleagues had ordered and could not eat. At least I avoided the mango and sticky rice which everyone else was spooning in to their mouths. However, on arrival back at the hotel, Areeya had magicked up a giant ice cream cake to celebrate Chris and Chow's birthdays, which both happened to fall on the same day. I went to bed bloated, determined to skip breakfast the next morning.

I don't recall much of the journey, or scenery we passed through on our way to reach Ko Jik. I'm sure it was hot, I mean interesting. The last part of the journey involved taking a small boat out into the estuary. Once we had loaded our gear, the boat chugged along for about an hour, finally reaching the small island where we were going to spend the night.

I was pretty much dreading this, as I do not share the romantic notion others have, of getting away from it all. I envisaged bug infested, small, badly ventilated rooms along with antiquated and inaccessible bathroom facilities. I suppose this is an age-related thing, as when I travelled in India and other countries in my 20s and 30s, I was quite happy staying in various dives, where any kind of bathroom or toilet facility was considered luxury.

On arrival at the homestay, I was not surprised to find that the rooms we were to sleep in, had no air-con or attached bathroom. However, I was pleasantly surprised, on further investigation, to discover that there were four bathrooms on the ground floor, so ample facilities really. I had a torch so the prospect of numerous nocturnal visits was not too daunting. My resolve to not drink that evening faded quickly.

After settling in, which simply meant checking the fans worked, I took an exploratory walk, intending to go around the whole island, which I was told should take about an hour. On the way I spotted a couple of pleasant looking, small hotels which I was sure would have air-con and en-suites. After about 20 minutes I gave up on my exploration and made my way back to our homestay.

There was only one area to sit and, as the evening progressed, and more beer was drunk, the conversation inevitably turned to armchair philosophy. I expounded my theory that we all have what is known as a resting face. The look our facial features naturally take. For some people, many in fact, this is an inane smile, exuding positivity. That is not the case with me.

. . .

My resting face is one of abject misery and negativity. I might say, this is because I'm constantly lost deep in thought, cogitating on the great mysteries of life.

This led me on to observations of my travelling companions. But I kept these to myself, until now at least. In essence they were not a bad bunch. A number of them were English in the extreme; unable to countenance drinking anything but tea in the morning and even then, not without milk. This required Areeya making sure she had purchased some milk from 7 Eleven the night before. Milk is not commonly consumed in Thailand, except by kids. Also, although the male contingent had grasped the concept of using a spoon to eat pad thai and fried rice, the ladies seem unable to move away from chasing small serves of their meal around the plate with a fork. And boy, did they love to chat. Every plant had to be observed in great detail so, when we were all ready to set off after a short break, they would begin discussing the minutiae of a small plant lying by the roadside. Chris had plenty of experience of such laggards and simply said:

- *OK, we're off,*

and counting

- *1, 2, 3,*

so that he and Areeya began pedalling the tandem in sync - he'd set off. Eventually the chatty ones would catchup.

. . .

That night, as expected, I slept fitfully. At first it was too hot, despite the fans blowing noisily across my supine body. Later as the temperature dropped, enabling me to doze off, I would still wake, like clockwork, every two hours and pad across the rickety, planked flooring, to the bathrooms.

Escape from Alcatraz

*Day 7 – Ko Jik Island to Trat – 38km
biking, elevation gain 365m*

The next morning, I was happy to leave the homestay and even happier to discover that, instead of another hour-long boat trip, this morning's sea voyage was less than 20 minutes, to a point on the opposite side of the estuary. As I later discovered, it was to be the toughest biking day of the entire trip, due to some short but steep hills. We started with a five-kilometre boat ride to the village of Ang Ka Pong. On landing, the climbing started straight away as we had a 40-metre ascent from the village. We then followed small roads past Trat airport and ascended again to the Khao Ra Kam Reservoir. Finally, some flat riding as we biked along the edge of the reservoir. Although the terrain was flat, there wasn't really a road. Just a gravelly path, liberally scattered with rocks and boulders of various sizes. I rode carefully and managed to avoid any accidents.

. . .

Others were not so careful and at least one person took a tumble, fortunately at a slow speed, only suffering minor cuts and bruises. As we passed a small dam, Chris announced the option of a minor detour, to see a Buddha statue built at the edge of the reservoir. The statue was visible only when the water level in the reservoir was low, which it should be during the dry season. An ancient Buddha staue was located here before the reservoir came into existence, which explained the unusual location of the present-day Buddha.

As this, not-to be missed spectacle, involved a couple of steep hills, Manu and I decided to walk the kilometre or so to it. The sun was blazing from a cloudless sky and the air was still. After a few hundred metres, Manu decided to turn back. Feeling the need for spiritual healing, and relishing a short time alone, I continued. I walked along the well laid out path, relishing the occasional respite from the heat, as I passed under small trees which afforded, if only for a few seconds, some shade. The only sounds were the birds and my own deep slow breathing. I arrived at a small intersection just as the others, who had ridden to the statue, appeared. The road split here with one track leading downhill again towards the statue. It didn't look that impressive and I decided it was certainly not worth walking down the hill to see it, knowing that I would then need to walk back up the hill to join the main road. I admired the view from afar for a moment or two and then walked back towards the main road. A couple of trucks passed and I tried hitching a lift but was unsuccessful.

. . .

Most of the way back to join the others was downhill and I arrived at the designated meeting point after a pleasant, contemplative, 10-minute stroll. We set off again on our bikes. From this point the route became more or less flat. The road was quiet, passing through forests and rubber tree plantations. After a stop at a 7 Eleven, we arrived in Trat city and checked into our canal side resort in the city centre.

Look at Trat

Day 8 – Exploring Trat – 21km biking, elevation gain 106m

A full day in Trat today. We visited two temples, a museum and a couple of monuments. All dedicated to King Taksin, who's a pretty big cheese around these parts.

In the evening, everyone else leapt on their bikes for a trip around the local lake. We'd already completed part of this route during the day and I did not feel I needed to do it again. I stayed at the hotel and arranged to meet the others at a designated restaurant for dinner. I spent some time deciding whether to walk or ride there. Eventually, I made the decision to ride to the restaurant and was glad I had, as it turned out to be further than I thought.

. . .

As we sat in the restaurant, I found the hard wooden seats were uncomfortable, so after 10 minutes or so I was forced to stand. In this position, and as we were approaching the end of our trip, I felt it was incumbent on me to make a short speech thanking Chris and Areeya. I waffled on for a few minutes, waxing lyrically about Chris's unbounded resourcefulness and Areeya's equally unlimited patience and kind-hearted attitude. We toasted the happy couple and were then ready to order our food.

Bangkok Traffic

*Day 9 – Travel day to Bangkok/HHH –
3km biking*

After a short ride to the bus station, we boarded a bus to take us back to Bangkok. We'd had to split up, as each bus could only carry four bikes. The bus I was on was fairly empty and after a couple of hours snuggled up against my seat partner Manu, I decided to move to the back, where there were plenty of free seats. Doing this reminded me of the halcyon days of the late 70s and early 80s when, not only was the music good, but you could pretty much always do this on any long-haul flight.

I'd taken a few snacks on board, but was looking forward to lunch. Around 2:00pm, which seemed very late for Thailand, we pulled off the main road into a large petrol station, which boasted a couple of pleasant looking restaurants and a 7 Eleven. The driver stopped his vehicle but didn't open the doors. He seemed to be engaged in conversation, through his window, with a youngish looking boy outside in the car park. After a few minutes we drove away and back onto the highway. We chugged along for another 45 minutes or so and then pulled up at a rundown looking establishment. The driver leapt out of his cab and disappeared, up to some nefarious deed I thought. A slightly ragged but friendly looking lady came out of the restaurant, saying to any foreigner within earshot:

- *20 minutes, come, come.*

Inside her establishment there were a few trays of not very appetising looking food and two large piles of fried eggs. All behind a glass partition. I pointed at the least unappetising looking concoction and asked:

- *anni phet mai* - is this spicy?

- *Nitnoi* - little bit, she replied.

She spooned some rice, an egg and a ladle or two of the brown food onto a plate and said:

- *50 baht.*

This was only around A$2.00 but I was fairly sure the Thai customer who had been served just before me was only charged 20 baht. I may have been wrong - they both end in *sip*.

I took a seat at one of the plastic tables and began to eat my food, which was stone cold. I ate the egg and some of the rice with a bit of sauce but really couldn't face the cold chicken dish, which was, unsurprisingly, more than a little spicy.

As we left the restaurant, the driver reappeared. He looked very happy and I couldn't be sure, but was he hitching up his trousers?

The bus rattled on. I dozed and listened to a podcast while following the route on my phone. We drove along Sukhumvit, the main arterial road that runs all the way from the Cambodian border, into Bangkok. Less than a kilometre from the Ekkamai bus station, our destination, the traffic came to a halt and we crawled the last few hundred metres of the journey. This was particularly frustrating for me, as we were following the BTS line and I could have asked the driver to let me out at pretty much any station, so that I could continue on the train much more quickly. But I didn't want to abandon my travelling companions.

Part Six

Quiet Days In Huay Phlu

Best Laid Plans

I'd changed my travel plans so that I could fulfil an appointment today with a contact at my old employer. He looked after corporate marketing and communications. I hoped perhaps he could help me get my previous books to a wider audience. But, at the last minute, I received a note cancelling our meeting. This was the third time it had happened. So, instead I arranged to meet another ex-colleague for dinner, and asked him to hand over my latest book, in an attempt to raise some interest in the Asian market.

After dinner at 8855 we repaired to Det 5, ostensibly for a quiet drink, but which turned out to be, what used to be called, a session. Having consumed a few beers with dinner, later in the evening, I'd moved on to red wine and my level of eloquence had increased exponentially. To me at least. As the drinks flowed, the conversation turned to literature. All I can really remember about the subsequent bavardage I had with my long suffering pal was my defence of the lengthy, heavily punctuated, sentence; the Dostoyevsky-Dickensian style, as I so succinctly described it. Probably more than once.

Going Up the Country

The next day I checked out of the Sawasdee hotel and booked a taxi to HHH. Instead of hailing one on the street I used the Grab app. Grab is the local equivalent of Uber which, for some reason, does not operate in Thailand.. I was interested to see how this would work out but there was no problem. The driver seemed keen to also bring me back to Bangkok. I wasn't sure why he thought someone would want to drive, in excess of an hour somewhere, and then come back straight away. I didn't really enjoy the trip much as the driver was one of those who sped up and slowed down all the time, with no apparent reason, thus bringing me to the edge of nausea. He was constantly on the phone and I think perhaps, in his defence, there was something wrong with his cab. I heard him graphically describing the frequent speed changes on the phone to his mates.

We eventually arrived at HHH and I checked in and soon recovered from the journey. After a short nap, I sat by the river for a while, continuing to regain my composure.

In the late afternoon, Chris and I rode to the market. Or rather, he rode and I tried to keep up. In fact, after a total of 14 days cycling, I managed quite well. Keeping up with Chris was always a challenge, especially so on this short excursion, as he was back on his own bike and off the tandem with Areeya.

We ducked and dived through the market picking up various items for dinner. At one stall a jovial lady, after asking 40,000 baht for some vegetables, then asked if I was married and before I could answer, said she wanted to be my wife. "One is enough", I replied, in Thai. Or at least I tried to.

I'd picked the wrong night to give up drinking as, after the 10-kilometre, high-speed ride in the afternoon heat, I was thirsty. Of course, I could have drunk water, or something else non-alcoholic, but when I opened the fridge in my room the glistening bottles of Leo were just too much to resist. Then when Chris told me that some other guests, who had checked-out that morning, had left behind half a bottle of wine, my fate was sealed. No drinking tomorrow.

Trains, and Trains, and Trains

The next day, after an early morning ride on my own, Chris and I set off for a visit to what he called "The Train Cafe". I had visions of an old train carriage which had been converted into some kind of eating and drinking establishment. Once again, Chris tried to ride slowly and I tried to keep up with him. He'd told me it was about 10 kilometres to the cafe so I expected it to be about 15. In fact, it was nearer 12. In the cafe we had a couple of coffees while I looked at a few model trains perched on shelves around the place. There were pictures of various trains on the wall. Nice, but not overly impressive.

Then the owner turned up and, after a short chat in Thai with Chris, produced an impressive looking bunch of keys from his pocket and led us into the inner sanctum. This was a barn-like room which must have been at least 50 square metres in area. Laid out and filling the entire room were various model railroads, all based on the actual rail networks in different countries of the world. We were the only visitors on the early morning mid-week visit, and the owner chatted enthusiastically about his project. The most amazing thing was the he had made all the small buildings, bridges and tunnels, of which there were hundreds, himself from cardboard and other materials he found lying around. Not from any kind of kit.

I asked Chris if the train enthusiast and genius model maker, was married. Surprisingly not. I thought maybe we could fix him up with the lady from the market who had proposed to me the night before.

One Big Fantasy

The end of the trip approached. I rose early the next morning and took a few pictures of the, always fabulous, sunrise over HHH. I had a cup of tea and then a short slow-paced ride into town. On the way back I stopped off at the Woodland Fantasy resort just down the road. The owner created this remarkable place himself. The cafe had been recommended and I went in for a coffee. Then I had a quick walk around. There was certainly lots of wood everywhere and the place sure was someone's fantasy. One large space was full of replicas of The Virgin Mary and a massive Jesus, suspended from a cross. In another area there were a couple of American Indians, native Americans or First Nations people - I'm not sure of the official term, also carved from giant pieces of wood. It was an odd place but intriguing and worth the time to visit.

One Big Fantasy

That's a lot of wood

Kids? - Nein Danke

The last day of the trip arrived. The Dutchman and his wife had stayed at HHH the previous night so we had breakfast together. I had booked a taxi for 11:30 to take me to the airport. As they were riding into Bangkok, I assumed they'd leave fairly early. But no, they stayed around for ever and only left just before me. I guess they enjoyed cycling in the heat of the day.

After an hour or so in the taxi, I wished I'd stayed in Bangkok the day before my departure and taken the train to the airport. The driver was OK, at least he drove smoothly, but the journey through the traffic-clogged streets was long and I fidgeted in my seat.

At the airport, I duly went through the processes of check-in and security, as I had many times before, then took a seat in a quiet corner, to wait for my flight. For the

Bangkok to Singapore leg, I had taken advantage of an offer to pay a small amount, A$10.00 I think, to upgrade myself to premium economy for the relatively short, two-and-a-half-hour flight.

I was soon pleased that I had, not just for the extra legroom and comfort, but because, back in Economy I could hear a small child who screamed for the entire duration of the trip. In fact, when I changed planes in Singapore, I could still hear the little tyke at the gate where I was due to board my overnight flight to Brisbane. I was full of dread that he would also be on my flight and continue his wailing. But there was no sign, or, more importantly, no sound, of him once I had boarded. I guessed he must have been on another flight leaving from a nearby gate. I pitied the travellers on that flight, wondering how many of them would agree with my, *under 5? Please stay home,* policy, explained below.

In my darker moments I have a theory about people with children. It's unlikely to get much support. I maintain that anyone who has kids, should not be allowed to travel with them; indeed, leave the house at all, until their spawn is say, five years old. In my brave new world, this ruling would not be limited to flying. Given omnipotence, I would extend this edict to any public place; restaurants, cinemas, beaches.

Epilogue

Autumn Fall

A week or so after returning home, I went for a ride on my electric bike. How often had I dreamed of having this on the tours in Laos and Thailand. Since I had been away from Brisbane, a lot of construction work had started along the river. This made accessing the bike track I liked to follow more complicated than usual. I cycled along the road a little and then cut through a walkway with steps and a sloping path, which led down to the river. The path was really there for wheelchair users and, to avoid it being too steep, was designed as a series of shallow slopes with a curve every 20 metres or so.

Unaccustomed to the extra power afforded by the motor of an e-bike, and while negotiating the second curve, I pushed on the pedal a little and propelled myself against the small wall separating the pathway from the steps. This caused me to stop abruptly. I tried to put my foot on the ground to steady myself. But the ground wasn't there.

The slope meant that it was a few inches lower than I expected and I lost my balance, falling heavily to the ground. As is often the way with accidents, it all seemed to happen in slow motion. My right buttock hit the ground first, followed by my right arm. I lay silent for a split second or two, waiting for the pain signals to reach my brain. Nothing seemed to be broken, and as I slowly got to my feet, a friendly local who had been enjoying a cigarette in the sunshine, came to my aid:

- *Looks like you've hurt your arm mate*, he said.

I looked down but could see no obvious injury. Then I realised that my leg had blood on it. Blood that had dripped from the long gash, from wrist to elbow, in my right arm. I was shaking a little but bravely thanked the fellow and made my way slowly home, on foot.

The accident reminded me of the one Chris and Areeya had on the Friendship Bridge between Laos and Thailand. I felt that I had joined an exclusive club. But, in reality, I was already a member. I'd also fallen in a similar way, years before in Thailand. We were exploring a small island to the north of the city. Cars were not allowed so it was something of a haven for cyclists. I came around a corner and a small dog was blocking my path. I stopped and put my foot down to steady myself. But, on the edge of the path, there was a shallow gulley to catch water, so the ground was lower than expected. The laws of physics took over and I passed the point of equilibrium, crashing to ground.

. . .

It occurred to me that this had happened many times in my life. It happens a lot, both physically and metaphiscially. You need to stop for some reason, you try to put your foot on the ground, but it's not there.

It's a glorious, sunny, Sunday morning as I write this; safe and warm in my Brisbane apartment. Church bells are once again ringing in the distance. I'm wishing I was back in the saddle, panting and pedalling furiously, in a valiant effort to keep up with my fellow cyclists. Or, sitting alone in my favourite Bangkok bar. Perhaps later to be joined by a friend, maybe two, at my preferred Bangkok restaurant.

Or perhaps, bouncing along the rutted tracks of Laos with a Springsteen song blasting from the handlebar-mounted speaker, breathing in the dusty air.

The Germans have a word for this, *Fernweh* - a strong longing or desire to travel to faraway or unknown places. It is often translated into English as "wanderlust" or "itchy feet," but *Fernw*eh specifically connotes a feeling of homesickness for a place one has never been to and a yearning to explore and experience different cultures, landscapes, and ways of life.

About the Author

I was, as Groucho Marx said, born at an early age, in London (England). My parents moved to the Kent coast when I was seven. I caught up with them a year or so later. My school days were unremarkable. Some were marked but usually very badly. The only subject I had any affinity with was English and this was mainly because my parents both spoke it, often at the same time. My career has taken many turns, dips and troughs, a few false starts and even one or two emergency landings.

However, it seems I was destined for an eventual career in the travel industry. Following a failed attempt to make my fortune as a driving instructor, I joined British Airways as a Sales Agent where I stayed for 4 years before emigrating to Australia after marrying local girl Tracy. Fortunately for me this coincided with the rise of the CRS (Computer Reservations System) which later morphed in to GDS (Global Distribution System). I worked in Australia for a company called Galileo and in Europe and Asia for Amadeus. Both companies offered similar products and, obviously, both were best when I was an employee. I retired from the corporate treadmill a few years ago and I'm now officially an author.

My first book was **My Brother's Bicycle**. The story of two bike trips; 40 years apart, and some of the time in-between. All my other books have a recurring theme; travel memoirs with a dash of philosophy and healthy cynicism.

Cannes Encore! Travel in the Time of COVID

Les and Tracy had lived in The South of France from 1997 to 2007 before moving back to Australia via Bangkok.

So, when COVID began to release its grip on the world and airlines were flying again, they ventured out of their quiet sanctuary in Brisbane and boarded a plane bound for Nice.

Twenty-four hours later we were basking in the dappled sunlight of the Cote d'Azur.

But it wasn't all cheap wine and Salad Niçoise. There were inefficient bank managers and other bureaucrats to deal with. Not to mention noise-sensitive neighbours.

Cannes Encore is the story of two, not so intrepid, travellers and their exploits in the tourist traps of France along with excursions to other less travelled parts of Europe.

Partly together, partly apart, Les and Tracy discover the continent; each in their own unique style.

The Soft Nut Bike Tour of Burma

The Soft Nut Bike Tour of Burma was led by our friend Chris. Boundless resourcefulness and a refusal to accept defeat are just two of his many skills. Snapped chains, grinding gears and punctures are fixed in a flash and if it all gets too much for our less than youthful bodies, he'll conjure up a truck or train to get us to the next outpost of civilisation.

This book describes a ten-day tour of the less travelled area of Southern Myanmar. It's called the Soft Nut Tour because there was also a Tough Nut one which required a level of fitness and fortitude which we no longer possessed - if we ever did.

My Brother's Bicycle

A journey of contemplation and misadventure as I attempt, mostly unsuccessfully, to re-live a bicycle trip I first embarked on as a fresh-faced 20-year-old.

More than 40 years ago I headed south with a guy I met at Liverpool Street station in London.

Enfield to Athens on a tandem. They said it couldn't be done.

For the re-run I was better prepared, or so I thought. But as it turned out it didn't really matter.

Photos from the Road

The Dutchman and his lovely wife

Photos from the Road

One of many boats

Sunset somewhere on the road

Bumpy but not hilly

Pizza, beer, The Happiest Man Alive

Photos from the Road

Luggage loaded we set off across the lake

The group

Vegetable market

Not a vegetable market

Photos from the Road

Street scene

Areeya updates her Facebook page

Factory boat on Nam Ngum Lake

Live animal market in Vang Vieng

Two hours on a boat

Docking after crossing Nam Ngum Lake

www.ingramcontent.com/pod-product-compliance
Lightning Source LLC
Chambersburg PA
CBHW050309010526
44107CB00055B/2167